THE WORLD OF MUSIC

G. Wallace Woodworth

THE BELKNAP PRESS
OF HARVARD UNIVERSITY PRESS

CAMBRIDGE, MASSACHUSETTS · 1964

TO MY WIFE

CONTENTS

THE WORLD OF MUSIC

ᨠᨠᨠ PRELUDE

MUSIC in our day is a vast subject. It is not one subject, but many; not one field of activity, but dozens. Music is an art, a science, a literature, one of the humanities, and a field of learning. It is an area of education from kindergarten to graduate school, a craft, a business, an article of commerce. It is bought and sold. It is a powerful tool of the Madison Avenue advertiser, and it is an agent in propaganda. It permeates our life.

The young man or woman who loves music and wants to spend his life in it has, depending on the nature of his gift, the choice of a great spectrum of careers. There are composers, performers, conductors, scholars, scientists, librarians, radio and television engineers, critics, managers, teachers, and teachers of teachers. I make no distinction of value, no hierarchy of happiness, between the first and the last, or between the professional and the amateur. All may be equally devoted to and moved by beauty.

Our epoch, beyond all others in the history of music, is the age of the amateur, and not only the amateur maker of music, but, in countless numbers, the amateur listener to music. Never before have the interested and gifted nonprofessionals so far outnumbered the specialists. It is to these new members of the musical body politic that I direct this book, which grew out of a series of lectures on The State of Music given on the ancient foundation of the Lowell Institute in Boston during the spring of 1961. The lectures were aimed at the company of Boston citizens directly in front of me in the Hall of the Public Library in

Copley Square. To address a wider audience has required modification of presentation and elaboration of content. But the objectives remain the same. I am concerned with music as a part of what Edward Everett, in the first lecture ever given at the Lowell Institute, on New Year's Eve, 1839, called "the empire of the mind."[1]

It is my aim to touch upon the ever-widening orbit of music in the twentieth century and to reflect upon its impact on the life of ordinary people. I make no pretentions to completeness and no claim that I have surveyed the whole field and given a thorough and balanced account of music at mid-century. I have sought rather to be provocative in areas of broad and general interest, to call attention to evils, dangers, problems, and current issues, and to suggest some basic principles governing the pursuit of beauty in American life. Not alone the practitioners of music and the professionals, but the vast army of non-specialists will help, willy-nilly, to shape for good or ill "the age that is waiting before."[2]

"Culture is activity of thought, receptiveness to beauty, and humane feeling."[3] It is in the context of this opening sentence of A. N. Whitehead's *The Aims of Education* that I want to look at the state of music in our day. Do our multifarious musical transactions, commercial and scientific, meet the test of "humane feeling"? Do music making and music listening engage the mind in "activity of thought"? How general is "receptiveness to beauty"?

Beauty, first and last, is the subject of this book. In the arts, it is always the court of last resort. Whatever the issue or the condition in the practical world of men and events, the state of music can be measured only against its imperious laws. For beauty is as direct and unmistakable as the senses, as universal as mankind, and our deepest joy.

❧ CHAPTER I · MUSIC: BACKGROUND OR ART?

THE MOST notable single fact in the life of music in our own day is, to borrow a phrase from the vernacular, the "population explosion" in music listening. More people listen to music today than ever before in the history of the world. Countless thousands are concertgoers, listeners to live music; and, beyond the conventional pattern of recitals and concerts, there is the vast territory of the recordings and the limitless world of the air waves, filled with radio music and television.

An American music calendar issued in Washington as a part of the international People-to-People program, listed more than ten thousand music events in 979 cities for the 1960–61 concert season.[1] These included symphony concerts, opera, dance, chamber music performances, solo recitals, folk festivals, music workshops, conferences, and what are called by the ridiculous name "music clinics." The calendar boasts that 35,000,000 persons in the United States are actively interested in concert music. Compared with less than 100 symphony orchestras in 1920, we now have 1142—more than half the symphony orchestras of the entire world. These figures attest to the population explosion in listening. In the long history of the art, it is not the first. The opening of the first public opera house in Venice in 1637 brought opera to the people; prior to that, it had been an incidental entertainment for the celebration of a royal birthday, a princely marriage, or a coronation. The advent of the virtuoso orchestra in Mannheim in the eighteenth century and the erection of large concert halls in the nineteenth century attracted a new public to orchestral music. There was a wave of popular interest in "pipe organs" in the late nineteenth and early twentieth century. The Boston Music Hall organ became so famous that it made its way into that classic of homely humor *Artemus Ward: His Travels*.[2] The early music festivals, primarily choral, and the great Peace Jubilee in Boston, with its hundreds of singers and players and its gigantic audiences, represent another wave of interest; yet all these expansions of the listening public were specialized in appeal and small in the aggregate compared to the explosion of the middle twentieth century. From the first opera house in Venice to the Baths of Caracalla, from the Handel Festival in eighteenth-century London to Lincoln Center and the Hollywood Bowl, from princely birthday music to the ubiquitous community concert series, audiences for live music have been increasing. Radio and recordings have not dulled the excitement of the live transaction, nor caused a falling off in attendance.

What has been the effect of the new wave of listeners upon the general level of musical taste? This is the crucial question which will not only interest the historian of the future, but which must be of deep and immediate concern to all those who value the arts. Do larger and larger audiences presuppose a lowering of taste?

My own conviction is that any evidence of such lowering in public preference has been vastly exaggerated by timid, shortsighted, and greedy commercial managers. The repeated claim that the patrons of community concerts in the smaller cities and towns demand glamorous stars and programs made up of musical "gumdrops" is far from true. The new public spans the spectrum of society and education from the college graduate and ardent extension student, often well trained and experienced in listening and analysis, to the office girl and factory worker whose natural love of music finds in concerts and records the sustenance it has long sought. There are more of these lovers of good music than the professional managers believe; and they deserve far better than they get from many of the commercial promoters of music.

The network of Community Concerts, with managerial headquarters in New York City, is an example of the interdependence of music and business. Commerical organization and promotion have provided countless communities with a winter schedule of recitals and concerts which would be impossible to set up on an individual basis between independent artists and local management. Centralized management is a necessary and effective channel between local boards and the reservoir of artists. In this role it has an inescapable educational responsibility. Furthermore, I am convinced it is good business to broaden the repertory, introduce new music, and promote a wide variety of concerts, including such esoteric items as string quartets playing Bartok and vocalists whose specialty is Monteverdi, Purcell, and Bach. Yet many young artists report that their programs have been censored by the managers, who have "strongly advised," if not demanded an ultra-conservative repertory with its perpetual round of the music "the public knows and loves."

To elevate public taste is a slow process, but there is a growing sophistication to which the "good music" radio stations have contributed enormously. The education of public taste in the concert world is the joint obligation of central management, local committees, and the artists themselves. All three have shown too little faith in the public. The present narrow cult of the masterpieces will surely wane; and current evidence should encourage managers and artists to widen the orbit of concert music and especially to push forward into the new frontiers of contemporary art.

There is one *sine qua non:* managers and local boards and, above all, the artists themselves must believe in what they are doing. Forty years of personal experience with concert-giving and concert-going have shown beyond any doubt that the public will be receptive to the performer who is dedicated, heart and soul, to what he is doing and has the artistic mastery of his material. Only two things are required to win an audience—glittering craftsmanship and communicative power. These are the qualities that have opened up to the "ordinary public" the choral works of William Byrd, the concertos of Vivaldi, the operas of Monteverdi; and these qualities in performance will do the same for Machaut and Boulez, Josquin and Stockhausen, Ives and Carter, Webern and Kirchner.

* * *

In the technological world of the twentieth century the recording industry has gone through a cycle of transformations from the old wax cylinders to the discs played at 78 rpm, then long-playing records at slower speeds, high fidelity, stereophonic sound, and the magnetic tape. These rapid developments in recordings and reproducing instruments have opened up a territory far larger than that of the concert hall, and created a new empire of listeners.

Statisticians report that the gross sale of records within record clubs alone reaches a total of seventy to seventy-five million dollars each year, and that the membership rolls of the four major clubs include over 2,300,000 people.[3] The *Reader's Digest,* within a period of a year and a half, distributed two million copies of an album of "classical" symphonies, a total only slightly below that of a "popular" album.

The educational potential of recordings is unlimited for the listener who is curious about the long history of the art of music and its manifestations in the successive golden ages of the past. Regrettably, the catalog of available recordings is narrowed down to the late eighteenth and the nineteenth centuries, with few twentieth-century works and few records earlier than 1780. The commercial promotion of recordings has actually contributed to the cult of the masterpieces and the corresponding resistance to new music. How many recordings do you suppose there are of Tchaikovsky's *Fifth Symphony?* There is a new one every fortnight. It is a sad fact that the largest and most powerful of the record companies have been inexcusably timid, in comparison with the smaller companies, in recording and releasing controversial music of the twentieth century. There has been a similar timidity in the music publishing industry, with notable exceptions—such as the firm S. and N. Koussevitzky, which in the early years of the century brought out the works of Stravinsky, Prokoviev, and many of the most controversial composers of that time. There is unfortunately no counterpart to this in the recording industry, except for some small companies touched with idealism. Of all the programs of assistance for contemporary composers—commissions, subsidies, appointments as composer-in-residence—the most helpful would be the dissemination of recordings. A "first performance" in the concert hall is often the last; whereas recordings may be listened to repeatedly; and with familiarity comes understanding and appreciation.

The Baroque period has begun to be recognized by the commercial promoters, but the music of the galaxy of stars in the Renaissance, not to mention the fascinating literature of the twelfth, thirteenth, fourteenth, and fifteenth centuries, still remains a *terra incognita* for the record manufacturers. There is far more public interest in the twentieth century and in "early music" than the men of business believe. Their timidity, lack of enterprise, and concern for easy profits have drastically limited the educational role of recordings. The stock answer "we are in this business to make money" has its measure of realistic validity. My quarrel with the production planners in recording is that they have not only failed in "public service" to the art which gives them life, but have also disregarded a potential market in new fields where a large public is eager and waiting for their releases.

An example of callous disregard of public service in the name of business strategy is the practice of withdrawing from the record catalogs so-called "unprofitable" recordings, and removing them from the shelves, even when still available in quantity. The *Saturday Review* of February 25, 1961 lists 37 symphonies by Haydn, once recorded, but now deleted and discarded to make way for more profitable recordings. I suppose no more than 8 of Haydn's 104 symphonies are "best-sellers." But the lesser known works *were* recorded, and each one of them has its peculiar charm, its intrinsic beauty, and its value for a limited number of music lovers. Fashions change. There was a time when Haydn and the Haydn Society recordings were all the rage. Now Vivaldi, almost unknown in the record catalogs a few years back, has become a great favorite. There are two reasons for this popularity—the live performances in concert by the Italian string groups during the fifties and sixties, and the venturesome enterprise of the makers of the earliest Vivaldi records. Corelli and Sammartini and Alessandro Scarlatti are just as good, and could be just as popular. Vivaldi's star may dim; and are we always to be at the mercy of the latest fad? Surely it is not too great an economic disaster to preserve in the catalogs and on the shelves the already existing recordings from the more specialized areas of music history and literature, so long as the supply lasts![4]

* * *

If recordings have resulted in hundreds of thousands of new listeners, the size of the radio audience is beyond reckoning. But do they listen? Or how do they listen? And are they not a new race of men and women, altogether unknown and undreamed of in the world of music a few years ago?

Basically, there are two types of radio listeners: one, the voluntary and selective listener; the other, the involuntary, captive, and often unconscious listener. The ticket holders at concerts and the buyers of records presumably make their own selections, within limits set by the policy makers among the manufacturers; but those who become habitual listeners to the radio appear to be insidiously drawn into a network of perpetual sound to which they gradually become captive.

Here is the schedule of a radio station not many miles from the capital of the nation.

6 to 7	Music to wake up to
7 to 8	Music to eat breakfast to
8 to 9	Music to send the kids to school with
9 to 10	Music to dust by
10 to 11	Music to wash to
11 to noon	Music to iron by
noon to 1	Music to eat lunch with
1 to 2	Music to take a break with
2 to 3	Music to watch TV with
3 to 4	Music to keep kids quiet after school with

4 to 5	Waiting for father to come home music
5 to 6	Music to cook dinner by
6 to 7	Music to have dinner by
7 to 8	Good music
8 to 9	Other music
9 to 10	Music to do homework with
10 to 11	Music for lovers
11 to midnight	Music for tired lovers

All that remains is "Music to listen to music by"! Six in the morning until twelve at night—eighteen hours of uninterrupted sound. Or is it music? It's called music on the schedule, but it's not music to be listened to, but music to do something else to, or by, or with—music to be used, musical background, not musical art. There is one hour of "good music." What a lonesome violet in a field of weeds and brambles! The inference is clear: for good music, you really sit and listen, and you do nothing else but listen. In this timetable of horrors, there is some glimpse of the fundamental truth that music, or at least "good-music-seven-to-eight-P.M." is not background, but an art to be listened to.

The selective listener to the radio can of course have the Metropolitan Opera on Saturday afternoon, a number of symphony concerts, and many other good broadcasts.[5] The spread of the FM Educational Radio Network—desperately slow but still sure—adds, link by link, city by city, to the sum of first-class music on the air waves. But observe the following program from one of the best evening hours on the commercial networks.

1. MERMAN SINGS RAGTIME
   Alexander's Ragtime Band; Way Down Yonder in New Orleans; When My Sugar Walks Down the Street; Sweet Georgia Brown; After You've Gone
2. GOODMAN GOES CLASSICAL
   Concertino for Clarinet and Orchestra . . . Von Weber

3. LILLIE SINGS BALLADS
   a. The Waltz Song .... German
   b. Please Be Kind .... Cahn and Chaplin
4. BOLGER HIGHLIGHTS
   We're Off to See the Wizard; Life is Just a Bowl of
   Cherries; You're a Builder Upper; There's a Small
   Hotel; Ev'rything I've Got; The Old Soft Shoe

Although "good-music stations" are on the increase, and
public-spirited sponsors can be found to sustain a number
of excellent programs, the basic diet of the commercial
station remains an endless stream of inferior music from
"light classics" to hillbilly.

In the field of television we can be grateful for the Educational Network, the activities of the New York Philharmonic Orchestra and an occasional opera or ballet. Beyond
these few examples, television has done almost nothing for
the cause of music. It is a regrettable instance of the star
system that educational symphonic broadcasts have been
limited to the New York Philharmonic. Other orchestras,
other channels, and therefore other sponsors are long overdue. The sound of music on most television sets is abom-
inable. A vast amount of scientific research and development has gone into the visual department of television, but
the most magnificent de luxe screen is still equipped with
a speaker for sound which is entirely inadequate. And this
at just the time when the recording industry has moved
with expert scientific know-how in the direction of the
highest high fidelity!

*   *   *

The gargantuan monster of American technological and
entrepreneurial ingenuity is "piped audio," a form of instal-
lation which supplies perpetual musical sounds in public

places. Unlike the juke box, which, though a nuisance to those who prefer not to listen to it, requires the initiative of at least one listener and the tribute of an inserted coin to start it going, "audio" is ubiquitous. From supermarkets to subway trains, you cannot escape. Its promoters, the big businessmen of music, "take corporate pride in supplying some fifty million Americans daily with music which is meant to be heard but not listened to."[6]

The restless ingenuity of the entrepreneur knows no restraints when there is a new product to market. Here is a recent announcement from the press: "Dentistry goes hi-fi, as musical sounds eliminate sensation of pain. 'Audiac,' an earphone device which can be regulated at the dentist's will, plays jazz, classical, and children's music, includes a pain-killing waterfall sound for especially stressful moments."[7]

There has been talk of a closed-circuit radio system open to physicians only. A preliminary announcement in the *New York Times*[8] indicated that there would be thirteen hours of programming each day from 8 A.M. to 9 P.M. There would be two types of programs: selected music heard both in the doctor's waiting room and in his office; and three medical information programs to be heard only in the doctor's office. When first announced there was some doubt among physicians as to whether they could trust any existing organization to certify the programs of medical information or briefing, but apparently no one raised any question as to the choice of music for the thirteen hours of uninterrupted sound, so accustomed have we become to this background.

*   *   *

And so the listening population expands in ever-widening circles: the inner circle of concertgoers, small and select, yet in the millions; the larger circle of record players; the radio listeners and television viewers; and finally the inescapable bath of audio.

It is difficult to make a sober and balanced evaluation of the effect of these twentieth-century phenomena in communication engineering; and it is easy to go to extremes in praise or denunciation. There are widespread benefits and unlimited potentialities for good; and there are evils —insidious, positive, and frightening.

Let us look first at the evils. In this new world of canned music, whether records, radio, or audio, there are two things wrong: first, a great deal of the music is utterly inferior and worthless; second, the continued effect of background listening may be permanently damaging.

I have been amazed at the sound of the air conditioning system in many of our newest and best equipped halls and buildings—it is loud, and it is perpetual. We are surrounded by these sounds, day and night, and it is only a step from the air conditioner to background music.

It is the practice of radio stations to allow not one moment of silence between the first station identification in the morning and the final sign-off at night. Music, music, music, fading in and fading out, linking every item of news, every weather forecast, every advertising script, merging into an endless chain. Against that background of universal custom, how unique was the decision of WGBH and the Boston Symphony Orchestra to introduce radio silence during the fifteen-minute intermission of the symphony concerts. Instead of listening to "commentary between the halves," you are invited to take an intermission, just as the listeners in the hall are doing, and come back in fifteen minutes for the second half of the program. Why, in the name of all that is sensible, should not the radio listener be entitled to the pleasure of an intermission, as well as the live listeners? The answer is the tyranny of

blind radio custom and convention, and the more dangerous fact that radio listeners are only half listening anyway,
so insidious and habit-forming is the narcotic of background sound.

The flood of audio music in packages, to be played
softly, or not so softly, in the background of American life
has mounted like the waves of a hurricane sea. Starting
with the replacement of live dinner music in a luxury
hotel dining room, the audio industry has left us hardly a
spot where one can converse or think or read without
music. I have no quarrel with dinner music. A great deal
of fine music down through the centuries has been functional—the wedding march, the processional, the chorale
prelude, the Intonazione, the Divertimento, the Serenade,
the organ prelude and postlude, and dinner music from
Shakespeare and the great feasts of the sixteenth century
to the Strauss waltzes and Hungarian dances so characteristic of the hotel trio of yesteryear. Not all music is meant
to be listened to in respectful silence. On occasion talk and
music may even go well together. But there is good taste
and bad taste in dinner music, and there is a time and
place for everything. I have walked into a large college
dining room at 7:30 in the morning, to be regaled by an
indiscriminate mixture of background sound—"Some En-
chanted Evening," cha-cha-cha, a Brandenburg Concerto,
and a Brahms Adagio to accompany oatmeal and scram-
bled eggs, the morning newspaper, and breakfast conversation.

There is a delightful story of the public telephone booth
in New York, where, whenever you picked up the receiver,
even before dropping in a dime, you heard soft music
from no one knew where.[9] Workmen from the telephone
company finally located a wire which piped music into
nearby restaurants. The music had jumped from the audio

wire to that of the telephone connection, to the delighted amusement of countless listeners.

We are, in a subtle but insidious way, training an entire generation *not* to pay attention to music. William F. Russell, reporting on the college scene, wrote: "The students assemble notable sets of recorded repertory, start them on their turntables, and then settle down to their non-musical studies and general reading while the music occupies the subconscious background. One cannot telephone a student in his room without hearing some important classic in the background above which the student often has to shout into the telephone. But it is naive to conclude from this that we are having a great musical renaissance in our college dormitories. The person who can read abstruse philosophy while Beethoven Opus 131 is being played in the same room is not apt to become a sensitive listener to music. In fact he is training himself inadvertently in the opposite direction."[10]

Background music, especially of a supposedly soothing nature, has had wide use in therapy. Music therapy is a very large subject on which a great deal of research has been done by the psychiatrists. It is without doubt a blessed ministration in healing. But the specialized therapeutic use of music, by prescription, is something utterly different from the musical smog which overshadows much of our daily life. It would be my guess that the most beneficent ministrations of music would occur where it was possible to get beyond passive background listening into the area of active listening in which the imagination and the mind are both engaged and disciplined. Better still is participation in music through singing or playing.

One of the most outrageous misuses of music occurs when the arts are mixed and music is relegated to the background position in the very presence of another art. Some of the newer museums contain not only fine pictures well displayed but all the gadgets of modern technocracy, adding to such items as automatic atmospheric control and flexible lighting, a sound system with a battery of loudspeakers set into the ceiling for broadcasting music. I am told that the music emerging from these loud-speakers includes the most inferior stuff as well as the great classics. If the combination of poor music and great painting is in bad taste, the use of the classics—for example, Mozart's tragic *G minor String Quintet*—creates an impossible dilemma. Who really commands the attention, Mozart or Picasso? The human mind simply cannot do justice to these two sensory impressions at once. Bach, Mozart, Beethoven, Stravinsky resist the background.

Listening to music with half a mind—that perilous by-product of audio, radio, and records—is a danger which attends so excellent a modern development as large-scale outdoor concerts. When one observes the vast audiences for "music under the stars," or the thousands sprawled in parks surrounded with picnic lunches and cavorting children, one wonders what may be the ultimate effect on music in our time. Sun-bathing to Brahms' *Fourth Symphony* is a subtle encouragement of the wrong kind of listening, just because the pattern is so similar to many other semi-musical experiences which are half-time, half-attention, and less-than-half "receptive to beauty."

Consider the hi-fi addict, the proud owner of an "Astro-Sonic Stereo High Fidelity System" which "develops more than 100 watts of music power with solid state circuitry."[11] The man who is crazy about his "set" is apt to be far more interested in sound and sound effects than he is in music. Hi-fi and stereo have made an enormous contribution to the faithful reproduction of musical sounds, especially orchestral sounds. The sales-slogan catchword "high fidelity" implies a fidelity to the original; but its values are special-ized. Whereas its genius is to catch the full power and infinite variety of all sorts of sound effects, the small living room is not the place for it. The most perfect music for the living room is not the thundering batteries of the *1812 Overture,* but chamber music. I am not suggesting for a moment that we give up listening to the *Ninth Symphony* or Mahler's *Second* just because the small room is not the ideal place for their sonorities. Yet hi-fi and stereo at full volume, with lots of bass and treble boost, produces a great pool of sound into which too many listeners plunge for the sheer joy of swimming around. As one of my students said, such a swimmer is often washed clean of any ability to *think* of the music.

Recordings have been exploited and misused in adver-tising campaigns since the beginning of radio broadcasting. Even so distinguished and scholarly a society as the Amer-ican Association for the Advancement of Science has found a way to *use* music in its campaign for science education in America. An article covering the annual meeting of the Association in Chicago in 1959 reports:

ROCK 'N' ROLL CRAZE BOWING TO SPACE AGE

The rock 'n' roll craze has a competitor.

It's the "beep beep" school—music for the space age aimed at cultivating the interest in science of youngesters 6 and older.

Best sellers in the "beep beep" field include "Constellation Jig," "Planet Minuet," "Ballad of Sir Isaac Newton," and "It's a Scientific Fact."

A display of the music and records is part of the array of exhibits at the 126th meeting of the American Association for the Advancement of Science. . . .

The songs for the space age are part of the educational equipment devised by the Science Materials Center of New York to interest the nation's youth in science.[12]

There is an unchallenged notion, commonly taken for granted, that any sort of promotion requires the assistance of music to get it under way. I have heard, from one of our best educational stations, a serious program on Civil Defense which was introduced by a husky-voiced nightclub singer with a coffeehouse ballad on World War III. The speakers on the Civil Defense program were perfectly serious and businesslike. Why the cheap musical introduction?

Symphonic programs and opera on the radio are continually interrupted by commercial advertising, as the tribute exacted by the sponsor and blandly accepted by the great mass of the public. If that practice be a necessity in our radio and television economy, good taste and a sense of the fitness of things ought positively to forbid singing commercials in the sponsor's advertising on concerts of first-class music. If he must promote his product in a program of Beethoven and Brahms, let him do it in the spoken word without musical embroidery.

I have catalogued examples of the misuse of music because I am deeply concerned about this aspect of our contemporary life. The vast promotional operations of the music business, the misuse of music in advertising, the domination of the radio and television worlds by the all-powerful "ratings"—these are positive evils. Taste is molded by commercial controls. Even in the field of jazz, Billy Taylor reports that the better arrangements are rejected by the advertising agencies, who insist on the obvious, the simple, the "big beat."[13]

Viewing with alarm the new type of college examinations designed for scoring on IBM machines, a critic wrote: "The essential fact is that the introduction of the machine into any cultural area always forces the adaptation of the cultural medium to the machine. One of the invariable steps in this process is the shift of control to the technicians and the manipulators."[14] This shift of control in our musical culture from artists, musicians, and teachers, to businessmen, technicians, and manipulators is one of the dangers of our time. The former, the humanists, are likely to have a basic faith in people; the latter, the statisticians and the promoters, are apt to rate the least common denominator far too low in taste, thereby contributing to the further lowering of standards.

Advertising practices offer a discouraging example. Is there any valid reason, in all conscience, why the sale of records must be promoted by alluring pictures and the finest classical recordings encased in record jackets of the most atrocious taste in color and design?

Lack of faith in the public has spread even to educational television. In 1959, when I had the privilege of giving a course of twenty programs on the History of the Symphony, the manager of the station received a suggestion from the national headquarters of Educational Television that Mr. Woodworth, "relieve the constant demand of the program for the attention of the viewer by such devices as the presentation of nice-to-know rather than must-know information, anecdotes, and related nonmusical references."[15] I need not add that no change was made by the station or by me in the format of this series!

* * *

Despite all dangers and evils, there is, on balance, a bright side to the picture. Through recordings, radio, and television, we can sit at home and hear the world—everything from Romanian folk songs and dances from Trinidad, to Bach, Beethoven, and Bartok. A profusion of music, covering vast territories of musical literature, is at the immediate command of the happy owner of a record collection and a good player. The potentialities for education are endless.

There are many examples of the significant transition from an interest in the gadgetry of hi-fi to a real devotion to the finest sort of record collecting. And how many young people have graduated from a shelf of popular music to collections of symphonies, chamber music, the music of the Baroque, and so far as available, the music of the Renaissance and the twentieth century!

Through radio and recordings, music has spread far beyond the urban centers into the most remote countryside. Two ladies in Wallingford and Cuttingsville, Vermont, are the volunteer drivers of a musicmobile which peddles a lending library of records to one-room schoolhouses, village housewives, and remote farmhouses.[16]

Even background listening has, on the unimpeachable testimony of many persons, somehow or other aroused an interest which has ultimately brought music from the background out into the foreground of their concern. Good music stations, where blessed with enlightened and catholic tastes in programming, have introduced scores of new works to listeners who would never have encountered them if left to their own initiative in record collecting and concert-going.

The understanding of music, in any real sense, consists in responding to music in its own terms. This calls for active participation on the part of the listener. "Receptiveness to beauty" demands infinitely more than passive background listening. It challenges the utmost concentration on the part of the listener, and requires repeated hearing. Recordings make it possible to hear a piece, not once or twice in years of concert-going, but scores of times, over and over again. Some of my students amaze me; they know a Bartok quartet or a Vivaldi concerto literally inside out, because they have played it and played it.

The question whether the population explosion in music listeners is good or bad for the state of music hangs in the balance in our own day. We must measure music in radio, recordings, and television against its noblest and highest mission, "the fertilization of the soul." Insofar as twentieth-century inventions in mass communication have brought the art of music to millions to whom it was inaccessible before, we can be grateful. But where radio, television, recordings, and audio have debased the coin, forced music into the background, filled the sound waves with inferior drivel, and taught people *not* to listen, we should recognize this new age for what it is, not a blessing but a curse upon the art of music. It would be a sad day for music if the epitaph for our generation were to be "They have ears, but they hear not."[17]

All the problems raised in this chapter are problems in education—education in music, in listening, in taste, and in standards. "Receptiveness to beauty," in the philosopher's full meaning of that phrase, is the high goal. The education of the new population of listeners is the inescapable challenge. The army of teachers of music in schools must assume new responsibilities, never before undertaken, for the education of the masses. The record companies and the radio and television networks, must accept their civic responsibility and their obligation to the art of music. And the public, all those who love music, must insist that the new inventions of mass communication and mass distribution of music be used for good, not ill.

The goal is not musical education only, or even primarily, but joy, happiness, the stimulation of the imagination, the deepest delights in art. It is the paradox of art that enjoyment and regeneration go hand in hand. Stravinsky, in the

Poetics of Music, quoted Poussin: "The goal of art is delectation."[18] And Whitehead said in *Science and the Modern World:* "The fertilisation of the soul is the reason for the necessity of art."[19]

CHAPTER II · SCHOOLS, COLLEGES, AND CONSERVATORIES

THE TERM "music education" as commonly understood covers an enterprise gigantic in scope and diversity, complicated in organization, and controversial in aims and objectives. Implicit in the history of public school music in the United States is the lofty ideal of musical training for every child in the land. At the other end of the scale, music education must be concerned with the most gifted conservatory students about to join the company of performing virtuosi, and with Ph.D. candidates who are to be the learned scholars of tomorrow. In our national philosophy of free public education and infinite human mobility, music in the elementary schools must, by definition, minister to the needs of masses and, at the same time, nurture the talent of the most gifted young performers and the most superior scholars. There are 28,738 school districts in the United States, and each one is essentially an independent unit in the formation and implementation of educational policy.

The center of the massive machinery is the child, the individual, the human being. The process of his musical training ought to be envisioned as a continuous cycle, uninterrupted from the time he enters school until he graduates from college. This is normally a span of sixteen years of academic training; plus three or four more, making two decades in all. for scholars who go on for graduate work, or performers and composers who complete their training with a period of European study. Music education comprehends, therefore, kindergarten, the elementary and secondary school, public and private, and finally what is called higher education—the college and university, or the music school and conservatory.

Some idea of the vastness of the field can be gained from a list of the organizations of teachers which are active and influential in music education.

The Music Educators National Conference, the enormous organization of public school teachers, with a membership of more than 42,000 in 1963.

The National Association of Independent Schools, formerly the Secondary Education Board, with its Music Committee, active among the private schools.

The National Association of Schools of Music, an organization of conservatories and professional schools, including those college departments which are in fact, but not name, conservatories.

The Music Teachers National Association, which comprises the army of private teachers as well as many teachers in schools, colleges, and conservatories.

The College Music Society, formed of the merger of the Society for Music in the Liberal Arts College and the College Music Association.

The American Musicological Society, dedicated to research, scholarship, musicology, but composed largely of college teachers and occasionally concerned with problems of music education.

The International Society for Music Education, and similar groups in UNESCO.

Add the College Band Directors National Association, made up of school and college bandmasters, the American String Teachers Association, organizations of piano teachers and singing teachers, and others. The orbits of these various societies are not clearly defined, and there are overlappings of membership, of meetings, and of subjects treated in papers and publications.

The aim of each is no less than the typically American

ideal, the pursuit of excellence. In actual practice some are more content than others with the status quo. Movements for reform have often been retarded by the political and commercial interests involved in the great enterprise— state and local boards of education, school committees, state teachers associations, teachers colleges, music publishers, instrument manufacturers, even the costumers of marching bands and those who array *a cappella* choirs in their gowns of many colors. There has never been a time in the history of American music education when the spirit of reform was not in the air.[1] Strong forces in both public and private education, at all levels from elementary school to college and conservatory, are working diligently and persistently to improve the quality and raise the standards of music. Cooperation with these forces, whether isolated individuals or organized groups, is the order of the day for everyone with a concern for excellence, whether teacher, parent, college president, or lay member of a village school committee.

*   *   *

The history of American music education goes back to the Yankee Singing Schools of the eighteenth century, and to Lowell Mason who introduced music teaching in the Boston Public Schools in 1838. The reform movements of the twentieth century found one of their wellsprings again in Boston. In 1914, nearly a century after Lowell Mason, the Boston School Committee ordered a study of music in the schools and engaged a committee of musicians including Thomas Whitney Surette and Archibald Thompson Davison. The outcome of that association and that report was Davison's *Music Education in America,* and Surette's *Music and Life,* as well as the notable collection of song books called the Concord Series of Music and Books on the Teaching of Music in the compiling of which they were joined by Augustus D. Zanzig.[2] Surette's Concord Summer School of Music, likewise an outgrowth of the Boston Report, was largely concerned with the philosophy of music in the schools, the humanistic equipment of teachers, and irreproachable standards in music literature. For over a quarter of a century, until 1938, this school contributed to American music education scores of well-trained teachers with the highest ideals. I mention the Boston Report, the Concord School, and the Concord Series because their direct and indirect influence on education has been neglected by historians. Jacques Barzun laments the fact that "among the thousands who knew him [T. W. Surette] . . . there was apparently not thought or energy enough to produce a significant obituary".[3] The Concord Series contained no sight-reading exercises and no songs specially composed by the editors for the graded technical training of the pupils, an innovation which made it unique in its day. The choice of songs stressed the personal experience of beauty for the singer—the imperishable beauty of folk songs, rounds and canons, carols, chorales, simple madrigals, and easy partsongs from the Renaissance to Brahms. The series was truly the first of its kind. *The Harvard Glee Club Collection of Part Songs for Men's Voices* (from The Concord Series) pointed the way for a parallel reform in the repertory of college glee clubs which has been more widely recognized than the work of Davison and Surette in music for the elementary and secondary schools. Both men proclaimed a philosophy of "nothing but the best," in music to be sung and played in school and college, and insisted on professional standards—"musically realistic"[4]—in all the operations involving children and students.

If I have stressed the pioneer work of Davison and

Surette it is not to minimize the importance of other reformers and other centers of excellence scattered widely over the country. But are we today better off than we were fifty years ago? In all candor I must report that the picture is still very spotty. There are good schools where well-trained, imaginative, dedicated teachers are doing a good job; but there are great stretches of arid desert. It is possible that, if there were some way to arrive at reliable statistics, one might hazard the guess that the general level of music education has risen by 2 or 5 or even 10 percent the country over. I can report from my own experience with the Harvard Glee Club, the Radcliffe Choral Society, and the Harvard-Radcliffe Orchestra, as well as music majors and amateurs in my courses, that students on the average come to college better prepared in music than they did forty years ago. Leaving out all the variables in the equation, this reflects some measure of general improvement straight across the country. But there are sharp controversies among teachers about methods and materials, and a never-ending battle for higher standards.

In 1959 the American Council of Learned Societies appointed a committee to report on music in the elementary and secondary schools. This committee found several weaknesses. Too often the high-school music program was limited to bands, orchestras, and choruses, enrolling only those with performing talents and offering little or no instruction to 80 percent of the student body. The performing groups often overstressed entertainment activities, marching bands with drum majorettes, command performances for Kiwanis and Rotary Club meetings, conventions, and so on. The Committee made four recommendations. First, a basic course, described as "consumer music education" (an ill-chosen phrase), which should be required for one year and available thereafter as an elective. The Committee described this course vaguely as humanistic. Second, special programs in colleges and universities to train teachers for the new type of instruction in the schools. Third, a more "educational" attitude toward the rehearsals and activities of bands, orchestras, and choruses. And, lastly, suitable textbooks and materials, especially films. Existing teaching materials, said the Committee, were not adequate in the light of their recommendations.

A far more important report on music in the schools was the outcome of a two-week seminar held at Yale University in June 1963 as a result of the initiative of Jerome Wiesner, Director of the President's Office of Science and Technology, and the Panel on Educational Research and Development of the Advisory Committee to the Commissioner of Education in Washington. The thirty participants—composers, concert artists, jazz musicians, conductors, musicologists, university professors of music and of music education, and teachers in the schools—represented a diversity of professions never before brought together to consider the problems of music education.

The work of the seminar was concentrated in six areas: the teaching of music through writing, reading, and performing; the widening of the musical repertory of performing groups in the light of recent historical and ethnological research; the development of musical understanding through a study of music as a literature; the utilization of the composer- and performer-in-residence; the exploitation of new educational media, such as films, tapes, and programmed instruction; and the development of courses, resources, and activities for students who are more advanced musically and intellectually than their contemporaries.

The seminar may well mark the beginning of a new era in music education similar to that inaugurated by the Office of Science and Technology in the fields of science and mathematics. The chairman of the Seminar, Professor Claude V. Palisca of Yale, declared at its close:

There emerged a strong sense of commitment to the release of the innate musicality and creativity of school children, the development of a deeper understanding of musical processes, and to a musical repertory of the highest quality in every area of performance and listening.[5]

In my opinion as a participant, the Seminar sounded a new note of critical urgency and made an uncompromising demand for musical excellence.

*   *   *

The materials of music study consist of the textbooks and songbooks used in general music classes, and the music played and sung by bands, orchestras, and choruses. There is no excuse for anything but the best, at any level and under any conditions. It cannot be said that good music is difficult and poor music is easy, and that therefore one must start with poor music and move on to good music. There are unlimited quantities of the most beautiful music of great simplicity, from a spiritual like "My Lord, what a Mornin'," straight on to the choral theme of Beethoven's *Ninth Symphony,* from the song of a medieval minnesinger to a recorder tune from Elizabethan England.

Unfortunately, the lists of music published for choral clinics, orchestra workshops, and choral and instrumental state contests present for the most part a dismal array of cheap clap-trap. Recent Junior Festivals bulletins of the National Federation of Music Clubs reveal incredibly bad lists of contest music for girls' voices, boys' voices, mixed voices, junior and youth choirs. Speaking of inferior materials for school bands, Mr. Keith Wilson, conductor of the Yale University Band, has said: "Teachers or band leaders blame the music publishers for publishing only hack music for band and school orchestra groups, whereas the music publishers say they publish it because that's what the teachers buy, and much of the so-called good music stays on the shelves gathering dust."[6] The guilt must be shared by all.

The selection of music to be studied and performed is the most serious responsibility of those in charge of music education. All the problems of performance, whether vocal or instrumental—tone production, diction, tonguing, fingering, and all the rest, of all degrees of difficulty from simple to complex—can be illustrated in music of enduring beauty. The music class or rehearsal is the gymnasium in which youth exercises itself in the habitual experience of beauty; and this is true at any age, from little children in kindergarten through sixteen years of musical activity to the seniors in a college chorus or a conservatory orchestra.

The materials for the elementary and secondary music classes—that is, the songs for general singing—span the whole gamut of taste. Strange marriages between words and music have been arranged in the name of the learning process. The correlationists, those educators who steal precious school time from music per se to "relate" to people and to other areas of study, joined forces with the facts-and-dates teachers to produce the following, which is to be sung to a lilting version of "The Heavens are Telling":

> The father of the Symphony,
> The children loved we're told
> Papa Haydn he was called
> By people young and old,
> When over sixty years of age
> He wrote the Creation
> The great oratorio
> Known by ev'ry nation.

He was born in Rohrau, Hungary
In sev'nteen thirty two
And altho' his parents died
His friends were kind and true.
He lived at the time of Washington,
In Eighteen nine he died,
Remember Joseph Haydn,
Beloved far and wide.[7]

And this, with the assurance that "the theme used in this piece is from a Minuet by Beethoven":

When Beethoven was a boy in Bonn
Life was sad, his father cruel,
At thirteen his family was in need,
To help them all he worked and gave up school
But he's greatest of all in the classics
Written to inspire us,
Songs, sonatas and quartets for strings,
Concertos, symphonies, lovely things.[8]

Good taste is a most priceless and indispensable asset in the education of the young. In art, a false step, a compromise, and the bars are down. And, once the standards have been lowered, it requires twice the effort to raise them again. It is a crime to violate the tunes of Handel and Mozart, and an equal blasphemy to burlesque the American Negro spiritual. Because there are syncopations in the rhythm of the spiritual, it does not follow that the door is wide open for "jazzing it up" and decorating the harmony with exotic chords from the song hits. The arrangers of spirituals are guilty in the first instance, but schoolteachers cannot escape their responsibility for performing these Broadway versions with their jumpy rhythm and flashy endings. We may be thankful for the simple and authentic versions by John W. Work of Fisk University, whose father was one of the original group of Jubilee Singers. Within my experience, the public has never failed to be deeply moved by the truly "spiritual" quality of Professor Work's settings. It is never necessary to court applause with cheap and tawdry music.

Public performance is an important factor in the activities of school choruses, bands, and orchestras. As a college choral conductor I have observed that, although occasionally accidents and tension mar the results, normally the culminating *educational* experience with a beautiful piece of music comes at the concert performance. It is then, as never before, that concentration on the music is at its highest among all the singers; and the reward is frequently an experience of profound beauty. There is every reason for a schedule of concert performances as objectives in school work. There is every reason also for the natural pleasure and excitement of singing and playing for others. To be sure, the ACLS Committee was right in pointing out the danger of too many entertainments by band, orchestra, chorus, or other musical groups, which take them out of their educational orbits. Only the teacher is the judge of what constitutes a reasonable schedule.

As there has been overemphasis in physical education on public spectacles in athletics, so in music there has been gross overemphasis on competitions. Aside from the philosophical objections to contests in art (which I shall discuss in Chapter VI), there is the practical objection that many of the contest pieces are of little musical value except as tests of technical virtuosity, and that the urge to win encourages the expenditure of too much time on a limited number of pieces.

The medical term "clinic" (and, worse still, "clinician"), so widely applied to a choral festival and its visiting conductor, puts the emphasis all in the wrong place—not on the musical experience, but on the pathological details of performing technique. Joint performances are good; competitions and clinics often do more harm than good. There is little educational value in an army of high school students assembled to compete with each other, chorus against chorus, band against band, like football teams. How much more rewarding is an occasional joint performance with two or three schools, not more, in which each performs several pieces, rather than one contest piece, and then all rehearse and perform together a few larger works, quite possibly beyond the resources of each individual school!

One of the more recent developments in school work is the activity called counseling, and the related field of testing. Counseling has become a full-time, specialized profession; it has been taken out of the hands of the regular teachers who used to "advise" their students in the course of their everyday work. Much can be said for this new profession, but a counselor cannot know everything and, since he must advise scores of boys and girls, he often relies on mechanical tests. An impressive number of reports indicate that counselors in general are woefully ignorant about music and that students are channeled *out* of musical activities and courses into other fields through inexpert or thoughtless advice.

There are grotesque, but true, stories of talent tests administered free of charge by the manufacturers of instruments. In such cases *everyone* is talented, especially for the instruments manufactured by the company administering the test! There are stories of the organization of school bands by dental examination. Look at the teeth of the children, and their jaw formation, and select those "dentally gifted" for the band, and let the rest take up the violin or cello; or select for the violin classes those whose little finger on the left hand is of proper and adequate length! Educational testing and measurement has become a profession by itself, and a commercial business as well. There is a long and important history of tests in music, starting many years ago with the celebrated Seashore tests, but some of the most important things cannot be measured, and blind faith in "scientific testing" has led to tragic errors. The proliferation of tests and measuring devices, with their electric computers and IBM machines and mysterious alphabetical and numerical scores, have been applied to the mind of the child to prove his ability or lack of it. The polysyllabic jargon continues to multiply—"response sets," "multidimensional judgments of desirability," "forced choice format items," "unidimensional continuum"—all irrefutably scientific and guaranteed to produce "highly reliable scores."[9] Tests and measurements have made their contribution to American education, but we have over-emphasized these dramatic programs which require large segments of time and large outlays of money. At best the tests can measure scraps of information and items of fact. You cannot sum up with the IBM machine the rigorous self-discipline, the opening of the windows of mind and heart, which comes with the study and performance of great music.

An activity in music education, thought by some to be on the periphery, and by others to be absolutely central, is "creative music." This has taken two forms. The older advocates of "creativity" insisted that the child should construct his own instrument, should play on no others, and should be denied the making of music until his instrument was satisfactorily finished. The newer school, promoted especially by the music faculty at Bennington College, though with wide-spreading roots in various practices in the past, believes that music can best be taught and understood by encouraging and guiding the student in the invention of compositions for voices and instruments, and then by rehearsing and performing these compositions as the basic exercise of the music class. The conservative view of activities such as the construction of a makeshift instrument or the writing of compositions has been summed up by Thomas Munro, who referred soberly to the careless use of the term "creative" in current education:

> One of the approaches to art . . . is sometimes called "creative." I would prefer to reserve this eulogistic term for the few cases which really deserve it: those involving some important, original contribution to the world's artistic heritage . . . Children's work in art is often spontaneous, in the sense of being done without direct imitation or guidance. This does not make it "creative" in the fullest sense.[10]

The finest statement I know of the case for creative activity in composition comes from the Summer Institute for High School Music Teachers sponsored jointly by the American Council of Learned Societies and Bennington College in 1962. It was drafted by Lionel Nowak, Henry Brant, and the sixteen high school teachers participating in the Institute.

> Composition is the starting point of all musical activity; and as such it should be the first step in the acquisition of basic musical insights. It provides strong motivation for musical curiosity, it is an incentive for the investigation of varying styles and systems, it develops analytical powers necessary to the astute and properly satisfying perception of any musical experience. The student must be encouraged to range as widely as his imagination will allow in the composition of music meaningful to him. His point of departure should be the present world of sound; his scope of understanding and application will gradually broaden to include usages of a growing past as well as experiments for the future. A constant reference to great works in the musical literature will help develop a sense of discrimination. As compositional development proceeds, the

student becomes aware and appreciative of the reality of harmonic, contrapuntal, and formal values. These heretofore narrowly defined and narrowly taught disciplines can now assume a rewarding validity which is not possible when they are declared to be antecedent to composition. . . .

The teacher must be a highly skilled musician with diversified areas of musical competency. Specifically: He must have developed skill in the techniques of composition, arranging and transcribing; he must have a wide knowledge of compositional ideas and devices. This knowledge must not be limited to the past, but must include specific understanding of the workings of twentieth century systems, structures, and media.[11]

The final paragraph recognizes the need for gifted and specialized teachers. I have seen something of the Bennington program and find it highly stimulating, but its successful application depends upon a qualified teacher, rare in the profession. Truly gifted first-class conductors of chorus, orchestra, and band are scarce enough; master teachers of history and literature are in short supply; even rarer are those equipped by bent and training to achieve something significant and valuable in creative music. It is easy to make a counterfeit of creativity. Nonetheless, pioneer programs in the field should be encouraged where a faculty can be found to teach the teachers!

* * *

Before leaving the multifarious and engrossing problems of music in elementary and secondary schools, I should like to return to the first recommendation of the ACLS Committee—that basic instruction in music history and literature be added to the high-school curriculum. The committee attached to this area of study the questionable title of "music for consumers," a phrase borrowed from the vocabulary of marketing, to point up the contrast between the "manufacturers" of music—choruses, orchestras, and bands—and those who make no music, only listen to it. They referred to the hegemony of the performing organizations in school music and to the lack of musical instruction for those who do not perform. I would state the case far more strongly. All children, performers and non-performers, need instruction in listening to music. Music is a literature, and music can be studied just as literature is studied. Music is an art, and music can be observed just as paintings are observed. Music literature ought to be the culminating study in the musical program of the schools, rather than the poor stepchild.

The study of music literature calls for listening as well as performing, and listening which is active and disciplined, not passive. From kindergarten to grade 12, the ear and the mind need musical training as well as the voice, the fingers, and the embouchure. The goal is what Whitehead has called "receptiveness to beauty," and the method is "activity of thought."[12]

At all levels, time should be devoted to listening as a regular part of the music program, under the guidance of a music teacher with proper equipment. Rigorous training should aim to counteract the vast amount of background "audio" which has engulfed our society since the invention of recordings, radio, and television. Music should be brought into the foreground, as an end in itself and an intellectual discipline, not as a background to eating, conversation, or homework.

The content of listening periods requires thoughtful attention and a fresh approach. The best teaching is now done in the kindergarten and elementary school where music is listened to *with* action—walking, skipping, dancing—thus opening to the child the whole world of rhythm and movement, of music which does not convey other than musical ideas. All too soon, however, the listening experience in school narrows down to pictorial and "story" music, mostly of the nineteenth century. There is nothing wrong with the "Carnival of the Animals" or "Peter and the Wolf"; they are delightful pieces. But they are often "taught" in the classroom like a musical fairy-tale picturebook, and they help to inculcate the notion that music must always convey ideas outside music, and ideas "adaptable" to the young. By contrast, little children are exposed to poetry which they cannot possibly understand but which they can deeply love, and great myths are part of the heritage of children in enlightened schools everywhere. Why not an equal representation of masterpieces from the main stream of western music?

At the high school level, the subject matter of listening courses should aim to challenge the emotions, stimulate the imagination, and engage the mind. Students in high school English classes come to grips with *Hamlet* and *Macbeth*, with *A Tale of Two Cities*—in short, with the most exciting dramatic and tragic works in the language. Beethoven belongs equally to the experience of the high-school student —the *Ninth Symphony* or the *Archduke Trio* or the *Emperor Concerto*. It is not the simple song forms and dances, the little examples of binary and ternary form, that really engage the mind and the emotions of a growing boy or girl, but the dramatic organization and impact of the symphony. The repertory of challenging music would eschew the *Nutcracker Suite* and a miniature gavotte or minuet, and would comprise, besides Beethoven, a Haydn or Mozart symphony, a Bach *Brandenburg Concerto,* Brahms' *First Symphony,* a Tchaikovsky symphony, and a large work of Stravinsky, Copland, or Honegger. I need not call the roll; each teacher will make his own way through the literature.

Those high schools which have a music teacher with

solid training in the history of style and analysis, should offer an elective course in the symphony, or a comparable body of literature—not an over-all survey from Gregorian to twelve-tone music. The survey can be left to the colleges. There need be no textbook—in fact it is better if there is none—but the assignments should involve listening to records, and the classes should become laboratory sessions, as in physics or chemistry, for detailed analysis.

The aim is not scraps of information, an aggregation of facts, nor any attempt at a balanced and comprehensive grasp of music history; it is to provide training in active and analytical listening. Analysis involves exactness and refinement of hearing. As in a science class, the teacher should be forever asking the student for an accurate description of what takes place; and the ear, not the eye, is the observer. The main "topics" for study should be drawn naturally out of the music itself, and should include such items as the sonorous qualities of the several orchestral instruments and choirs, the texture of chamber music, individual peculiarities of style in composers represented in the assignments, and, most important of all, the manipulation and development of musical ideas.

A basic distinction must be drawn—at all ages, from grade one through twelve—between music which is "about" something—program, pictorial, or delineative music—and that which conveys none but musical ideas. Both have a vast literature and I make no distinction of value; but it is the latter which is most frequently neglected, whereas it is far more effective in inculcating "activity of thought" in listening. A close study of the manipulation of musical ideas in a symphony, so often regarded as complex and forbidding, is one of the easiest aspects of musical practice to observe, simply because, in its context within the dramatic grand plan, it challenges the mind and engages the emotions. Such training of ear and mind is not only a good general preparation for college music study, but it is also an end in itself of the highest order in the educational program.

Let me summarize the three great objectives, as I see them, for the next decade in American secondary schools. First, the introduction and proliferation of such courses in music outside performance, as I have just described— courses in listening and in music literature. In some high schools, one such course might be required for all students in a given year, following the general music course in the first eight grades. Other courses would be among the electives. These listening or literature courses should deal at all levels with music that challenges the emotions of the children, stimulates their imagination, and engages their minds.

The second great need is an offering of specialized courses in both the history and the theory of music for those gifted or interested children to whom the school also has a responsibility. Mr. Conant, in his first report on the American high school, recommended that "*All students should be urged to include art and music in their elective programs,*" and later on: "All students should be advised to have as the central core of their elective programs significant sequences of courses."[13] Courses in music theory, as well as in history and literature, constitute what Mr. Conant calls "a significant sequence of courses." The only limitation upon such specialization would be the capacity of the music staff, the availability of the necessary teaching materials, and the requirement of a reasonable balance in the program of study.

Rigorous courses in theory or literature should be given entrance credit for admission to those colleges where counting course credits is still a practice in evaluating candidates.

Extracurricular musical education, involving participation in performing organizations or outstanding talent in an instrument or singing, is to an increasing degree taken into consideration by those admission committees which seek to evaluate "the whole man."

The third great objective is to attract to the field more and better teachers. As the final recommendation in his series of proposals for the Junior High School, Mr. Conant said: "The superintendent and the principals *must* [and he underlined *must*] recruit a competent teaching staff, for on the quality of the teachers, in the last analysis, all depends."[14] With the improvement in music instruction in college for the amateur as well as the professional, and with the profound educational experience of participation in excellent college glee clubs and orchestras, one may look for better preparation and higher standards of taste from the general classroom teacher, to whose ministrations music must be entrusted in the lower grades. The prospective music teacher or supervisor would be well advised to take full advantage of the A.B. program of liberal studies, instead of concentrating too heavily on professional skills. A five-year program of preparation, generally styled Master of Arts in Teaching, is more realistic than the attempt to crowd teacher education, professional training, and liberal studies into a four-year sequence. The tendency of NCATE (National Council for Accreditation of Teacher Education) to overstress education courses at the expense of the student's major field and of general education should be resisted.

Historically "music educators" (a term applied exclusively to public-school music supervisors and teachers) have been a race apart. "Very few of our distinguished composers, performers, or critics have ever contributed" to the development of school music.[15] Not from choice, but by force of circumstances, the educators have worked in a measure of isolation. Departments of music education in conservatories and colleges have been too much separated from the regular music program. Every avenue should be explored which will bring the spheres of school music and art music closer together.[16]

I shall return to teachers and teaching in Chapter VII, but let me point out right here that the most dangerous musician in the entire profession—in or out of school—is the magnetic, effective teacher whose own personal musical taste is defective. In a great gathering of high school children, I once heard an all-state chorus, a gilt-edged, gold-medaled choir. The program included Gabrieli, Brahms, Bach, and Randall Thompson. The diction was clear, the notes accurate, but everything was unspeakably dull. Then the chorus turned to some Broadway show tunes and immediately the music came to life, with animation, lilting phraseology, and superb motion. It was perfectly clear that the conductor had paid lip service to the classics and come into his own only when he hit the contemporary stage music. Here was a perfect example of a man of great technical competence and extraordinarily magnetic personality, yet he understood only one style which he had learned from the radio, the television, and the Broadway musical. The children told me afterward that they thought Gabrieli, Bach, Brahms, and Thompson were pretty dull. No wonder! Had the conductor understood the music of Gabrieli, Bach, Brahms, and Thompson, and radiated his own love for it as well as for the show tunes, the students would have followed him to the end of the world. This has happened thousands of times. It is a universal law of the teaching of art.

*　　*　　*

In the area of higher education, consider the student interested in music at the age of sixteen or seventeen. He has finished elementary school and secondary school, where his activities have been devoted for the most part to getting a good general education. Music has been a specialty or an elective, inevitably a peripheral subject outside the main core of his academic work. Now comes the fork in the road. Shall he go to college or to a conservatory? These words carry basically opposite connotations, but in recent years this polarity has become more and more obscured. Conservatories teach academic subjects, and colleges give credit for playing the piano. Institutions of learning at this level, no matter what they are called, reveal all shades of the spectrum, mixing academic and professional studies in varying degrees.

There is a positive virtue in simplicity. It would be better if there were a clearly marked fork in the road. Who belongs in the conservatory or school of music? Obviously the performer, the professional, the student who is looking forward to a career in opera, in a symphony orchestra or on the concert stage. And who belongs in the college and university? Obviously the amateur, the nonprofessional, the pianist who is not going to be a concert artist but a doctor, the amateur who doesn't perform at all but loves music and wants to understand it better. But certain music professionals also fall within the orbit of the university—the composer, and the scholar in music who looks forward to graduate school and research, and the teacher of music in schools, colleges, and universities. Both the conservatory and the college offer training directed specifically to the composer, and both are apt to have departments of music education.

If one considers the degrees granted, the distinction becomes clearer: in the college and university, Bachelor of

Arts, Master of Arts, and Doctor of Philosophy in Music; in the conservatory or school of music, Bachelor of Music, Master of Music, and Doctor of Musical Arts (or sometimes Doctor of Music). Yet conservatories call themselves colleges of music, and universities include schools of music and conservatories.

The older American conservatories started as informal associations of private teachers, awarding certificates or diplomas to their students.[17] European conservatories still devote themselves exclusively to singing and playing, and such professional training must remain central to those in the United States. Some blending of functions between university and conservatory is a historical inheritance, and apparently a permanent situation, but students planning to continue their music education beyond high school would be well advised to consider carefully the order of priority of their aims and ambitions—either a truly liberal education or a concentration on professional music study.

The most important trend within the conservatories in recent years is the increasing importance of group performance in orchestras and wind or string ensembles, opera workshops, and large or small choruses. Private lessons in singing and playing are complemented by instruction in orchestral playing and training in choral singing and in operatic production. Yet there is often conflict between the private teachers and the conductor of the orchestra or chorus or opera. Conservatory orchestras have become more important in the total work in the conservatory because instrumental graduates are far more likely to find their careers within one of the great orchestras of the country rather than on the concert stage as solo virtuosi. The path ahead for the singer is less clear.

The problem of the academic department in the conservatory is a problem of time and energy, climate and atmosphere. Courses in the humanities, language, literature, history, even philosophy and science have made their way into degree programs. This trend is fortunately being reversed. Neither enough time nor enough energy can be sacrificed from the main business of professional training to allow for anything more than scratching the surface in the academic field. The climate and the atmosphere of the music school ought to be professional, not liberal.

Departments of music education include sometimes as much as 50 percent of the student body of conservatories, and help to supply the ceaseless demand for more music teachers in the elementary and secondary schools. Both conservatory and college are equipped to provide an adequate basis for music teaching in the schools, though with divergent specialties. In the case of instrumental instructors, for example, it seems clear that the conservatory would normally have available a more complete offering than the college. In other fields such as history, literature, and analysis of music, the college is better able to meet the need.

The American conservatory and school of music has made a tremendous advance in the last century. It used to be thought that no professional musician was prepared for his work unless he had a period of European study. This is no longer necessary in the field of technical training, either in singing or in playing. Some of the greatest teachers in the world are here—Americans and Europeans—and the technical study of the instrument or the voice can be carried on just as well on this side of the Atlantic. A period of European study is important, not for technical training but for breadth of perspective and of culture. That, rather than intensive study of the voice or instrument, should be the goal of American music students who go to Europe.

*   *   *

Some years ago the National Association of Schools of Music appointed a committee on college work and the A.B. degree in music. The report of this committee, commonly known as the Cincinnati Report, is the finest statement of the broad outlines and basic philosophy of music in the liberal arts college. I have extracted some significant passages from this report.

1. THE NATURE OF THE A.B. DEGREE. The philosophy of the A.B. degree emphasizes the value and the basic importance of a broad education for all students, regardless of their eventual callings. The A.B. curriculum is therefore formulated with a view to a continuing exploration of various humanistic areas and scientific disciplines. It is expected that the student will devote approximately half of his time and studies to such work. . . .

Paralleling such studies, or, in some cases, following them, the undergraduate normally concentrates or majors in a particular field. . . .

Beyond this there usually remains a varying number of credits [courses] which are elective in nature and which may be employed to increase the degree of concentration in the chosen field, . . . or to explore subjects out of intellectual curiosity with no necessary view to a relationship within the major field.

Thus the doctor of tomorrow, and the lawyer, scientist, musician, linguist, teacher, and preacher are all expected to fulfill the same pattern of requirements, the basic aim of which is to create, in the best way possible, a literate and enlightened person. . . .

The degree of Bachelor of Arts with a Major in Music should be designed for three classes of students: (1) undergraduates who wish to major in music as part of a broad liberal arts program, but do not plan to enter music as a profession; (2) prospective candidates for the degree of Master of Arts in Music or Doctor of Philosophy in Music; (3) prospective school music teachers desiring a broad liberal arts education.

2. THE A.B. MUSIC CURRICULUM. The A.B. music curriculum serves two principal ends: A) to provide appropriate

courses for the general student, the non-music major; and B) to provide a thorough, disciplined training for the student who plans to make music his life's work.

A. THE NON-MUSIC MAJOR. In general, the needs of the non-music major are satisfied through courses devoted to studies of the literature of music, either by various categories, such as the symphony, opera, chamber music, song; by periods, such as the Baroque, Classic, etc.; or by composers or groups of composers. Such courses presuppose a high level of general literacy on the part of the students rather than a mastery of musical theory or a competence in performance. . . . In addition, the non-music major profits greatly by participation in performing organizations.

B. THE MUSIC MAJOR. All music majors, irrespective of eventual specialization, should devote the 30 to 40 required semester hours to certain common disciplines. In this way alone can a suitable curriculum be devised with the assurance that all majors will be exposed to the same intensive and broadening studies [in the technique or theory of music and in music history and literature]. . . .

4. APPLIED MUSIC. Applied music, whether taken with or without credit, on or off campus, is an essential part of any serious music curriculum. . . .

"Applied music" is taken to include 1) individual or group instruction in voice or particular instruments; and 2) performing organizations such as chorus, orchestra, band, and chamber-music ensembles.

The A.B. Committee has strong convictions about the important role of performing in the training of the music major (and the non-music major as well), but the committee has no particular brief as to how or to what extent individual institutions should credit applied music, if at all.

In this connection, it is appropriate to point out 1) that an important goal of applied music is to study the literature of music by means of performance; and 2) that an excess of credit hours assigned to applied music will inevitably curtail the opportunities of achieving the objectives stated at the outset [of this report].

The applied music recommended in connection with the A.B. would not be sufficient to train virtuosi, and the A.B. is not intended for such a purpose.[18]

The breadth and balance and logic of this report as a philosophical statement leaves no more to be said. Its clarity, workability, and practicality should commend it to the study of every music department in the country. It is a credo, and also a measuring rod. In a nation so large as ours there will be local variations, and they may well be quite justifiable. The Cincinnati Report remains a kind of basic constitution, a fundamental law for the guidance of faculties, deans, and presidents, and for the self-evaluation of departments of music.

One of the thorniest questions in college music has always been the matter of credit for applied music lessons and for singing and playing in musical organizations. Credit is essentially a measure of segments of time in a program of study, and indirectly a basis for tuition charges. It should never be thought of as a criterion of value. Arguments about credit based on a hierarchy of values are quite beside the point. Segments of time spent on practicing an instrument must be deducted from the total available for academic studies, and vice versa. It cannot be otherwise. The only question is a question of balance.

The majority of colleges and universities across the country have adopted some scheme of credit allotment for musical performance within a liberal arts program, thereby merging the applied with the academic. Students deeply interested in performance and at the same time eager for a liberal arts education are often reluctant to enroll where there is no credit for their lessons in singing or playing. Yet many of our best performers, as well as composers, have come from colleges where no such credit was allowed. There have been abundant examples of men and women in liberal arts colleges who took the full-time academic course, sometimes as majors in music and sometimes as majors in another field, and who found the time and the energy to continue their instrumental or vocal lessons on the side. What they wanted and valued was not some sort of division between credit hours in academic studies and credit hours in applied music, but a liberal college education in the arts and the sciences, with private lessons outside, *and* ample opportunities for performance under the aegis of student-controlled undergraduate musical organizations sponsored but not managed by the Department of Music.

Let me add a word of testimony from the situation that I know best, that at Harvard and Radcliffe. At the University we have six main performing groups with several hundred undergraduate members: the Harvard Glee Club, the Radcliffe Choral Society, the University Choir, the Pierian Sodality of 1808 (The Harvard-Radcliffe Orchestra), the Bach Society Orchestra, and the Harvard University Band, besides an opera group, a Gilbert and Sullivan Society, and House musical societies. No credit is given for participation in these activities; furthermore, they are managed and operated by students. Their policies are determined by the student officers in conjunction with the conductor. In only four of these organizations is the conductor a member of the faculty.[19] The very freedom and self-determination of these organizations is in no small part the cause of their success. Student responsibility combined with faculty leadership, not faculty domination, has been the secret of the great educational contributions made by these organizations in the musical life of the University for many years.

A remarkable development has taken place in the American engineering school recently—the rapid spread of education in the humanities and specifically in music. The Institute of Higher Education has published a study called *Liberal Education in Engineering* in which the statement is made that half the engineering schools in the United States should substantially increase the time allotted to the social sciences and the humanities. It suggests that a third of the curriculum in an engineering school should be devoted to the liberal arts, in this order of importance: English composition, economics, history, speech, literature, foreign language, and philosophy.[20] The work of the music department in the Division of Humanities at the Massachusetts Institute of Technology indicates that the list offered by the Institute of Higher Education should have included music—indeed should have placed it high on the roster. In these days of crash programs in science, the music department of MIT stands as an extraordinary evidence of the high regard of one of our foremost engineering schools for the particular contributions which music can make in a program of scientific education.

*   *   *

Music combines the educational values of a rigorous discipline and the communicative and regenerative powers of a fine art. This is the philosophical basis for all speculation on music education.

The Secondary Education Board, meeting in New York in 1959, devoted a series of sessions to the general subject "Discipline and the Disciplines," and the Music Educators National Conference, meeting in Chicago in 1962 under the presidency of Allen P. Britton, took as its subject for sessions lasting a week: "Music, an Academic Discipline." Discipline in music is part of what Whitehead calls the stage of precision in education.[21] In choral singing, for example, the discipline involves following the beat, perfecting the diction, mastering tone quality, control of dynamics, sensitive phrasing, good intonation, and, of course, the correct notes. Transactions so complicated as choral singing and orchestral playing serve as gymnasiums for the exercise of the most intensive discipline, which is manifestly self-discipline. The study of music literature through listening requires an equally rigorous training, but of the ear and the mind. Music, whether it be an elective course in harmony, or participation in the band, is one of the "subjects" most appropriate to the secondary school. But discipline is something more than any one of the specific disciplines. True discipline is indivisible, for it is the discipline of the whole self. It is a quality of mind, not just algebra or chemistry, counterpoint or trumpet playing.

In Whitehead's trilogy, the discipline of music is implicit in "activity of thought," whereas the communicative power of music begets "receptiveness to beauty" and "humane feeling." The tragedy of much miseducation in music is that the teachers do not have faith in children and young people. It has been proved hundreds of times that little children love music. They love music as sound and music as motion and rhythm. They respond to it in its own terms. They will sing the most beautiful songs if the teacher sings them first; and they will run and skip and dance in perfect synchronization with the propulsion and motion of music in time. They have no prejudice against the dissonance of contemporary music. They are far more curious and tolerant than their elders. The responsibility of the teacher is summed up in those awful words: "You can create or you can destroy." It is a universal law in art that the good will drive out the bad, that where great music is presented with as much excitement, imagination, and enthusiasm as poor music, young people will respond to the best. Receptiveness to beauty is one of the earliest characteristics of children, and unless it is snuffed out by exterior circumstances, it still lives in young people of high school and college age.

The problems of secondary and elementary schools are

the most massive and the most critical in American music
education. Yet there has been progress and there can be
more progress. The salt has not lost its savor and the leaven
is at work in the lump. Mr. Conant declared in *The American
High School Today:* "I am convinced that American
secondary education can be made satisfactory without any
radical changes in the basic pattern. . . . The improvements
must come school by school and be made with due regard
for the nature of the community."[22] School by school, here
a little and there a little—such is the only road to improvement.

The public at large has an inescapable responsibility for
the state of music in public education. The marked improvement
in college music for the amateur during the last
forty years must feed back to the local elementary schools
in the next decade, raising the level of taste and standard.
As members of school committees, members of parent-
teachers associations, or as plain citizens in the community,
those who care about music must never rest till they see
improvements in their own communities.

Music has been called a frill. When that taunt is leveled
at certain areas of American school music, we must in all
conscience admit the charge is valid. It is worse than a frill;
it is musical miseducation. But music, rightly taught, is not
a frill; it is one of the most powerful disciplines of mind and
personality.

Perry Dunlap Smith, former headmaster of the North
Shore Country Day School at Winnetka, Illinois, once
wrote me a letter about the connection between the general
spirit and morale of his school and the condition of the
music department. "Now that the work in music is uncertain and not on an even keel, the whole morale of the
school has changed." Music, in his educational philosophy,
was the ideal avenue through which his students could

satisfy needs which Mr. Smith felt to be paramount—the need to experience beauty and the need to express emotion. "All the avenues to the soul must be kept open all the time." The young boy and girl need the stimulation of the imagination and the discipline which is "not distinct from enjoyment but by reason of it."[23] These great gifts the imaginative and dedicated teacher can bestow.

CHAPTER III · MUSIC IN CHURCHES

TO UNDERSTAND the state of music in the churches requires some knowledge of the breadth and scope of three separate areas—the history and literature of church music, its basic philosophy, and its practical administration. Each is a large subject in itself. Yet any discussion of church music calls up facts, notions, convictions, and problems, drawn severally from each of these territories.

Church music, for the musician and the music historian, is an enormous body of literature. At certain periods it embraced nearly all the written music of the time, and there has been no epoch, even our own, without its significant contributions. It has a continuous history stretching back in an unbroken stream to its known sources in the fourth century of the Christian era, with even more remote springs in the unrecorded music of the early Christians and the Psalmist of the Old Testament, King David. As a result of the spread of historical knowledge through schools, colleges, and recordings, more people than ever before are beginning to be aware of the extent, the variety, and the beauty of this literature, and to recognize the contribution which so vast a treasury might make in services of worship.

Church music is not only a history and a literature, but also an area of philosophical and theological debate. In the narrowest sense this is related to liturgics, but in a broader sense it touches on aesthetics and psychology as well as theology. It is a battleground today, as it always has been, where thoughtful (and sometimes thoughtless) people con-

front each other in what has been satirized as the war
department of the church. Arguments on its philosophical
problems take place not only in learned volumes by theo-
logian and scholar, but also at Everyman's dinner table on
Sunday noon, where the battle rages over the organist's
tempo for the last hymn, the tremolo of the soprano soloist,
or the case for or against Bach Chorales.

In its practical aspects, church music involves a whole
area in the administration of a parish: organ music, choir
music, congregational hymns, weddings, and funerals. Except in the meetings of the Society of Friends, music has a
part in nearly every act of public worship.

Our historical position today is not that of the pioneer
on the border of a new frontier; nor are we at the culmination of a long development. We stand, rather, in the middle
years of a great movement of reform. Some of the reformers
are musicians, the organists and choirmasters of the
churches; others are clergymen, and still others ordinary
laymen in the pews. Discussion of the problems of church
music, whether casually at Sunday dinner, or more ear-
nestly among clergyman, choirmaster, and music committee,
requires more acquaintance than most of us have with the
history, the literature, the philosophy, the standards of taste,
and the practical issues involved in the use of music within
the church.

*   *   *

The history of church music in this epoch of reform
begins with the years 1903 and 1906. In 1903, Pope Pius X
issued his *Motu Proprio,* a decree designed to regulate the
administration of music in the Roman Church.[1] In 1906,
the Oxford University Press brought out *The English
Hymnal* with Ralph Vaughan Williams as the musical

editor. Reform was in the air among both Catholics and Protestants.

This was not the first time. The entire history of church music is a history of alternate abuses and reforms. Church councils have labored with the problems from medieval times. The Lutherans, the Calvinists, the Puritans, the Quakers—each sect had its philosophy. Thoughtful men, from popes to humble laymen, have pondered the impact of music, an art of sound and motion, upon the offices of religion.

The *Motu Proprio* of 1903 is the most important single document in the history of church music in the twentieth century. It aimed to abolish the "secular" and often theatrical style which had been on the increase since the eighteenth century. It ordered the restoration of Gregorian chant, to be performed in the churches according to the practice of the monks of Solesmes. It singled out Palestrina's style as the model for polyphonic church music, and admitted modern compositions only if their style was sober and in keeping with the liturgical function of music. It limited orchestral music to special occasions, and restricted the organ to simple accompaniments. The tenor of the *Motu Proprio* echoes a letter issued by the vicar of Pope Leo XII in 1824 which states unequivocally that "nobility and seriousness of style must characterize all music to be performed in holy places, whatever may be the occasion."[2]

The mere promulgation of an edict does not mean that the regulations on church music will be universally observed. For the faithful the edict ought to be absolutely binding in conscience; yet the practical exigencies of the situation intervene. The philosophy may be clear, but a lack of knowledge of the history of church music and of its literature, together with sheer incapacity on the musical side, render the decree ineffective. The Pope himself recognized that "a shameful and inexcusable ignorance" would interfere with the observance of his regulations.[3] On Christmas Day, 1955, Pius XII issued a supplementary encyclical devoted exclusively to the subject "the discipline of sacred music." Here he attacked the all-important question of education among the clergy. "Great care must be taken that those who are preparing for the reception of sacred orders in your seminaries . . . are properly instructed in the doctrine and use of sacred music and in Gregorian Chant according to the mind of the church, by teachers who are experts in this field."[4] The most authoritarian of ecclesiastics cannot by legislation or decree bring about reform —it comes only by instruction in both the "doctrine" and the "use" of sacred music.

The appearance of *The English Hymnal* represented an attack on abuses in hymnology, a narrower field than that embraced by the Pope in 1903. Yet Vaughan Williams' Preface sounds the same clear call for reform.

The task of providing congregations with familiar tunes is difficult; for, unfortunately, many of the tunes of the present day which have become familiar and . . . popular with congregations are quite unsuitable to their purpose. More often than not they are positively harmful to those who sing and hear them.

The committee believe that many clergymen and organists are now realizing their responsibility in this matter, and will welcome a tune-book in which enervating tunes are reduced to a minimum. The usual argument in favour of bad music is that the fine tunes are doubtless "musically correct," but that the people want "something simple." Now the expression "musically correct" has no meaning; the only "correct" music is that which is beautiful and noble. As for simplicity, what could be simpler than "St. Anne" or "The Old Hundredth," and what could be finer?

And at the end of the Preface, the solemn declaration: "It is indeed a moral rather than a musical issue."[5]

"Time would fail me to tell of Gedeon and of Barak,"[6] to

call the roll of the great twentieth-century reformers. They were the colleagues and followers of Vaughan Williams, men like Percy Dearmer and Robert Bridges in England, Canon Douglas in the American Episcopal Church, Henry Wilder Foote in the Unitarian Church, and many others. One of the most persistent and effective was Archibald Thompson Davison, who gave two series of Lowell Lectures in Boston on Church Music, in 1935 and in 1940, and was the author of two powerful books, *Protestant Church Music in America* and *Church Music: Illusion or Reality?*[7]

One of the strongest forces in the battle for higher standards consists not of musicians but of laymen, amateurs, nonprofessionals, who have become sensitive in matters of taste. An ever-increasing number of men and women who have sung Bach and Palestrina and William Byrd in school and college find themselves impatient with Barnby, Dykes, and Dubois in the church. The improvement in school and college music and the dissemination of good music by radio and recordings have contributed enormously to reform in church music. There is a new generation of clergy and laity who are well aware of the riches of musical literature, and are better equipped than their elders to pass judgment on the quality of hymns, anthems, and organ music. This presents a challenge to the church and to church musicians. In the Preface to the *Pilgrim Hymnal* of 1959, Henry Sloane Coffin states the issue squarely: If young people "grow up to despise what was given them in the house of God, either in words or in tunes, their respect for the Christian church is seriously enfeebled."[8]

In church music as in school music the only effective strategy in the campaign for reform is the gradual process of education. Reforms are not accomplished by fiat, nor on a nation-wide or denomination-wide scale. Only church by church, choir by choir, hymn by hymn, will a more worthy, dignified, and noble music supplant inferior offerings in the worship of God. The more enlightened clergy, laity, and musicians must work together to carry forward those reforms instituted in the opening years of the century.

* * *

Turning to the deeper levels of philosophy behind the practices of church music, I should like to state, quite simply, my own credo. I believe that music has no validity in the church except as a symbolic form or avenue for the worship of God. I have the greatest respect for the traditional practice of silence among the Quakers and for their positive distrust of the evils and hazards of musical performance within the meeting house. A similar warning of the dangers of music comes from the Clericus of the Potomac Convocation of the Episcopal Church: "Music can be an effective aid to devotion and a fitting agent of the word, but it is not essential to public worship, and can be an obstruction unless it is properly selected and executed."[9]

I believe that music, "properly selected and executed," is a corporate expression of worship through the art of word and sound. Under worship I understand the expression of praise, adoration, wonder, awe, prayer, penitence, thanksgiving, trust, hope, and sacred joy. The mission of music and words through all time has been to put these reverent attitudes and these deepest feelings of man into formal artistic expression, and to release them as a corporate offering or sacrifice.

Music is the handmaiden of worship, "an help to devotion." I take this beautiful phrase from a discourse on church music by William Beveridge, Bishop of St. Asaph at the end of the seventeenth century.

And therefore they that sing only with the voice, and not with their hearts, had even as good hold their tongues. And they that come hither only to hear the organs, had as good stay away. For whatsoever I have said concerning church music, be sure it will avail them nothing, that come not with a hearty and sincere desire to serve and honour God. For music is only an help to devotion; and therefore, they that do not truly endeavor to perform their devotions to God, cannot possibly have any help by it.[10]

If music is in truth a corporate offering to God himself and "an help to devotion," then it must represent our best fruits—an art of inherent excellence, dignity, and musical integrity. In the deepest sense it must be pure in heart.

We must recognize the existence of unworthy music and of irreverent and shockingly secular performances. As in the field of school music, we must confront the positive force of evil. It is ridiculous to pretend that there are no standards of excellence within the structure of art itself. There is no place in the church for bad stained glass, sloppy prayers, cheap jokes and laughs, and slang in the pulpit. And there is no place for shoddy, inferior, unworthy music in the choir loft. It is a sin of blasphemy.

On the Saturday morning before Easter Sunday, and again at Christmas, the New York Times prints a full-page announcement of music programs for the New York churches. It is a depressing commentary on the state of church music. After fifty years of musical evangelism, the majority of the anthems performed at the great church festivals are undignified, sometimes musically illiterate, and often patently secular. Survey the complete repertory for all the Sundays of the year in many churches and you will find far too great a proportion of anthems calculated solely to show off the choir and to entertain the congregation.

I have referred to the criteria of music worthy to be offered to God as a corporate expression of worship, enumerating artistic excellence, integrity, and beauty. What about the question of a sacred as opposed to a secular style? There are some who would say that nothing "worldly" is fit for the art of the church. It is clear that at some periods there has been a conscious attempt by composers to differentiate sacred and secular style, and it is true that such music as Gregorian Chant, by its very strangeness to modern ears, presents an image of other-worldliness. But it is equally true that there has been at times a merger of sacred and secular style—for example in Handel, Bach, Mozart, and Brahms. Bach, who wrote no opera, composed dialogues between the Soul and God full of romantic tenderness and in the style of the secular Baroque duet. The example of Bach, however, is no warrant for the excesses of *verismo* opera or for the introduction of the waltz, the march, or the cloying harmonies of song hits.

Some music in the contemporary idiom is eminently suited to the uses of worship, as is the polyphony of the sixteenth century, the peculiar *a cappella* sonority and diatonic harmony of traditional Russian Church music, and the modality of the English and Italian schools of the twentieth century. By their uniqueness and consistency of style as well as their dignity and austerity, they appear to the modern ear antisecular.

I would not be inclined to lay down strict guide lines between sacred and secular style, even if it were possible; but I would draw widely on the varied literature of church music of past and present, measuring each item with infinite concern for the excellence of its craftsmanship and the communicative power with which the music enshrines the sacred text. To the organist and choirmaster, and to the clergyman, both of whom are inextricably involved in the transaction of church music, I say: "Let your conscience be your guide," but I add: "Be sure your judgment is informed and your heart is pure." St. Paul said: "I will pray with the spirit, and I will pray with the understanding also: I will sing with the spirit, and I will sing with the understanding also."[11] The choice of music for the solemn act of corporate worship requires both the spirit and the understanding also.

I have deplored the curtain of sound which the radio and packaged audio have draped over the whole of the American scene.[12] This is at its worst in those churches where perpetual and ubiquitous sound fills every moment except the sermon. I have seen an order of service in which "organ response" appeared fifteen times—after the invocation, after the first lesson, between the prayers, after the announcements for the week, after the invitation to the offering, after the sermon—never once a moment of silence. Frequently the minister requests that the organ be played softly during the prayers, with the result that the sacred words of the liturgy, the approach to the throne of grace, are accompanied by maudlin harmonies on the voix céleste or unda maris. More than once, as University Organist at Harvard, I was asked by visiting clergymen to play quietly during the marriage ceremony, as though at that most sacred moment when man and wife take their vows the simple and beautiful words are not enough. At a famous cemetery outside Los Angeles, music is broadcast perpetually from loud-speakers hung in the trees. Should not the dead sleep in peace?

A curious incident which has had minor repercussions in the field of church music is reported in the following news account:

On October 13, 1957, the British television audience was offered a live broadcast from St. Augustine's Highgate, where the communion service was being celebrated, it appeared, in a new fashion. Whatever was said by the solemn ecclesiastical gentleman who opened the program could hardly have prepared the viewers for what came next. The cameras swooped around to reveal a baritone, a small vocal group reminiscent of those employed to record singing commercials, and a full-fledged dance band, complete with saxophones and high hat cymbal.[13]

This was the first performance of *A Twentieth Century Folk Mass,* composed by the Rev. Geoffrey Beaumont. There has been some specious talk about how the old masters wove popular tunes into their Masses, so why not jazz in the Communion Service? Viewed against the backdrop of the deepest spiritual expressions of secular as well as sacred music, this jazz Mass is no more than an isolated vagary. It owes its fame to the obvious news value of its sensationalism, and to the fact that it was recorded, thus attaining some circulation as a curiosity. There have been few actual performances either in England or America, and there are no signs that serious composers intend to follow this excursion into jazz church music.

* * *

The relation between the minister and the musician is of primary importance in the practical day-by-day operations of music in the church. It is not always recognized that the ultimate responsibility for music in the church rests with the minister. The organist is his deputy and his assistant. If music is to be "an help to devotion" and an offering to God, then the minister cannot avoid his responsibility, and the organist and choirmaster should always recognize it. All too common is an easygoing division of authority in which the minister says in effect to the organist, "You are the expert in your field; you go ahead with the music and I will take care of the service and the sermon."

The responsibility of the clergy is spelled out in detail in the canons of the Church of England and the American Episcopal Church. The 1959 revision of the Anglican canon law is explicit:

1. In all Churches and Chapels, it belongs to the Minister to direct when the organ shall be played or when it shall not

be played, and to decide what parts of the service shall be sung.

2. Where there is an organist or choirmaster the Minister shall pay due heed to his advice and assistance in the choosing of chants, hymns, anthems, and other settings and in the order of the music of the Church; but at all times the final responsibility and decision in these matters rests with the Minister.

3. It is the duty of the Minister to ensure that only such chants, hymns, anthems, and other settings are chosen as are appropriate, both the words and the music, to the solemn act of worship and prayer in the House of God, as well as to the congregation assembled for that purpose; and to banish all irreverence in the practice and in the performance of the same.[14]

And Canon 24 of the American Episcopal Church reads:

It shall be the duty of every Minister to appoint for use in his Congregation hymns or anthems from those authorized by the Rubric . . . and, with such assistance as he may see fit to employ from persons skilled in music, to give order concerning the tunes to be sung in his Church. It shall be his especial duty to suppress all light and unseemly music, and all irreverence in the performance.[15]

If this be the responsibility of the clergy, explicit in the Episcopal Church and implicit in those churches where it is not spelled out in the canon, then it follows that there is an equal responsibility for training in music in the theological seminaries and divinity schools. Within the last fifty years in the United States, provision for such training has increased to a marked degree. Nearly all theological schools now offer regular courses in church music for seminarians. To find time for this instruction in the crowded schedule of the divinity school—which now involves such new subjects as psychiatry, social work, and counseling, as well as the older and more traditional disciplines—has been a real problem. However, the instruction in church music during the last twenty years will bear fruit in the next decades. Already, in an ever-increasing number of churches, the raising of standards has come as a result of the initiative and intelligent administration of the clergyman.

The minister and the organist are colleagues. In many churches the musician has been given the title Minister of Music. This correctly describes his function, and is typical of our modern literalism. Whether Minister or Choirmaster, the office has honor and dignity, and the ancient title calls to mind a long succession of dedicated servants of God, including Palestrina and Gabrieli and Bach and hundreds more, a veritable cloud of witnesses hovering over the choir loft.

The clergyman is the indispensable ally of the choirmaster. If the latter has thought through the philosophy of music as the handmaiden of worship, there ought to be the closest association between the minister and the musician, with a mutual understanding of the problems involved on both sides.

There exists in many churches a music committee. If the only job of the music committee is to hire and fire the organist, then it had better be abolished. If, however, the music committee looks upon itself as an ally of both clergyman and choirmaster, then it might well change its name to "committee on worship." This has happened in a number of churches, and the change in descriptive title is significant of a reformed view of the place of music in worship. As colleagues of minister and choirmaster, the members of this committee on worship ought to hold regular meetings with them, in the hope of being helpful at every point in the problems and operations of the musical organizations within the church.

One of the most troublesome areas in the field of church music, an area which demands the cooperation of minister, organist, music committee, and frequently the financial administration of the church, is the matter of the organ, its care and possible replacement. Churches are always buying new organs, and frequently they abandon a traditional pipe organ for some new electronic gadget. There is a great deal of misunderstanding here. People in general know very well that a Stradivarius violin made two centuries and a half ago is just as good now as it was when it left Stradivarius' workshop. The actual fabric of the organ, the organ pipes themselves, do not wear out any more than a Stradivarius violin wears out. Unless the pipes have been very badly mistreated they are just as good today as the day they were made. The mechanical part of the organ deteriorates—the bellows, the console, the keyboard, the mechanical connections. But that which makes the sound remains untouched by the ravages of time. Furthermore, the nineteenth-century craftsmen did their work with infinite skill and devotion, and many an organ built between 1860 and 1890 is a far better instrument than a twentieth-century organ, let alone the as-yet-imperfect electronic instruments.

It is gratifying to observe an increasing interest in the surviving older organs, many of them outstanding in beauty and value. The Organ Historical Society, a new organization with rapidly increasing membership, is dedicated to the preservation of old American organs. Many of them are to be found in small village churches scattered throughout the country. This is a work of reclamation, but how infinitely better to repair and restore one of the gems of 1880 than to throw away a perfectly good organ just because it is "old," and install in its place a radio-station or night-club electronic instrument with its synthetic sound and eternal tremolo!

The Organ Historical Society published in the January

1961 issue of its periodical, *The Tracker,* a list of fifty-two old organs now for sale in the eastern United States—the earliest built in 1831, the latest in 1899. One example among many of a still earlier age is an organ built by John Snetzler in London in 1762, orginally set up in a church in Boston, then moved to South Dennis on Cape Cod in 1854. It has recently been restored and is in excellent playing condition, a beautiful survivor of the eighteenth-century art of the organ builder.[16]

*   *   *

Congregational singing should occupy the central position in church music. It is more important than the performance of expert choirs and virtuoso organists. Leadership in hymn singing is the responsibility of, first, the clergy and, second, the organist and choirmaster. Over a century ago Henry Ward Beecher declared in the Preface to *The Plymouth Collection of Hymns and Tunes:* "We do not think that Congregational Singing will ever prevail with power, until *Pastors of Churches* appreciate its importance, and universally labor to secure it. . . . The pastor should . . . be the animating center of the music, encouraging the people to take part in it."[17]

The hymns should be chosen by the minister, not by the organist. The clergyman cannot delegate his responsibility in this major area of the service of worship. However, there is every reason why the organist and the minister should cooperate in the choice of hymns. The organist, after carefully studying the hymnal, might well make a list of inferior hymns, to be avoided whenever possible, and a similar list of excellent hymns, many of which, alas, are unknown in our churches although available in the hymnals. These hymns should be repeated until, if at all possible, they become as well known and well loved as any of the "old favorites." Dr. Raymond Calkins, minister at the First Congregational Church in Cambridge, used to follow the practice of assigning a "hymn of the month." This was a new hymn, or an old hymn which had been neglected, and which he announced every Sunday for a month. If the congregation still sang it badly, he scheduled it for four more Sundays; if at that point it still seemed not to have made its way, he and his organist were willing to abandon it, at least for the time being.

In the performance of hymns, much depends upon the leadership of the organ itself, the solidity and firmness of the tempo, and the devotion of the choir in leading the congregation. Choirs should be reminded that the singing of the hymns is one of their most important functions in the church. "Hymn sings," and rehearsals of hymns, outside the regular morning service, scheduled as a late afternoon or evening service, would be helpful in educating the congregation in the riches of the hymnal, especially if the minister or the organist or both were given some opportunity to talk about the history and the beauty of hymns and of congregational singing.

In 1761 John Wesley set down his *Directions for Congregational Singing.* Two centuries later this historic statement remains equally valid as a warning against common errors and a guide to good performance.

SING ALL. See that you join with the congregation as frequently as you can. Let not a slight degree of weakness or weariness hinder you. If it is a cross to you, take it up, and you will find it a blessing.

SING LUSTILY, and with a good courage. Beware of singing as if you are half-dead or half-asleep; but lift up your voice with strength. Be no more afraid of your voice now nor more ashamed of its being heard, than when you sing the songs of Satan.

SING MODESTLY. Do not bawl, so as to be heard above or distinct from the rest of the congregation—that you may not destroy the harmony—but strive to unite your voices together so as to make one clear melodious sound.

SING IN TIME. Whatever time is sung, be sure to keep with it. Do not run before nor stay behind it; but attend close to the leading voices, and move therewith as exactly as you can; and take care not to sing too slow. This drawling way naturally steals on all who are lazy; and it is high time to drive it out from among us and sing our tunes just as quick as we did at first.

ABOVE ALL, SING SPIRITUALLY. Have an eye to God in every word you sing. Aim at pleasing him more than yourself, or any other creature. In order to do this, attend strictly to the sense of what you sing, and see that your heart is not carried away with the sound, but offered to God continually; so shall your singing be such as the Lord will approve of here, and reward you when he cometh in the clouds of heaven.[18]

The life of a particular hymnbook is normally no more than one generation. Every twenty-five years, on the average, there is a new edition, involving the gradual retirement and disappearance of both words and tunes, the introduction of new hymns, and the restoration of beautiful hymns from the treasury of the past. From time to time new hymnals appear, like *The English Hymnal* of 1906, which was called forth by the imperfections of the old hymnal of the Anglican Church, *Hymns Ancient and Modern*.

Marriage, divorce, and remarriage between words and tunes has been common practice in hymnals. Tunes are classified by their meter—Long Meter, Short Meter, Common Meter, 7.6.7.6., etc.—and are interchanged at will among texts of the same metrical organization. This fact of history and practice is often forgotten by those who cling to "association," as though these marriages were set up in heaven. Some texts, like "Now thank we all our God," seem indissolubly wedded to a single tune, but this is not the normal situation. Association is a strong force—for good and for ill—over the period of a generation, but it should not be thought to be permanent. Vaughan Williams' tune "Sine Nomine," a new setting in 1906 for the words "For all the saints," has by mid-century universally replaced the older Victorian tune, equally universal for many years.

1861 was a crucial year in the history of English and American hymnody. Ten years earlier, in *The Hymnal Noted,* John Mason Neale had combined for the first time Gregorian chants and English texts. In 1855 *Lyra Germanica* had enriched English hymnody with many of Catherine Winkworth's classic translations of German chorales. *Hymns Ancient and Modern* (1861) was an eclectic book, drawing on the two great streams, Gregorian Chant and Lutheran Chorale; but it also let loose on the churches the flood of Victorian hymns which even today, a century later, are warm favorites with certain groups in our congregations. This inferior musical tradition, which accounted for so large a proportion of tunes in the older hymnals, has been eroded, slowly but steadily, in the stern winnowing of time and taste. The good has driven out the poor. I venture to say that not more than a dozen tunes will make up the ultimate and final harvest of permanent value from the second half of the nineteenth century.

Although it has been said that the time is ripe for a new era of hymn composition, the twentieth century has produced few new tunes. Possibly the general character of contemporary music is antithetical to the genius of congregational song. The general improvement in hymnals, one of the most notable facts in the church music of the twentieth century, has resulted from adopting the musical policy inaugurated by Vaughan Williams in 1906—to deal sternly with the inferior tunes of the nineteenth century, replacing them by treasures drawn from the past. Texts of various origins have been remarried, and with great success, to Gregorian Chant, the "Songs" of Gibbons, the Genevan, English, and Scottish Psalter Tunes, and folk songs from many countries—strong, sturdy, and eminently singable.

Marriage and death are moments when human considerations should, in my opinion, take precedence over musical factors. Given the closest cooperation between clergyman and organist, inferior and undignified music can probably be avoided, and the strong stand of the Roman Catholic Church has gone a long way to improve matters in this regard. On the other hand, requests for special pieces to be played or sung at funerals or weddings are often fraught with the most intense personal feeling. I shall never forget the series of Navy weddings at which I played the organ during the Second World War. Oftimes they took place just before the beginning of active duty at sea. The young couples wanted to be married in the Harvard Chapel, and with music, though there was only a handful of guests and family and friends were too distant to attend the ceremony. My organ library contains a collection of horribles which I played without question at the request of the bride or groom. That was no time for a course in music education. I take the same stand about requests for music at funerals. I have heard of a funeral at which the "Blue Danube Waltz" was played, because it was the favorite music of the deceased, and of another which included a vocal solo called "Good Night Here, and Good Morning Up There." I have myself played "Pomp and Circumstance," because the mother of a dead soldier felt it struck so triumphant a note at the close of the service for her son.

If good taste and high standard be compromised at the

merciful prompting of sympathy and humanity, let it be only on such rare occasions. In the normal year-round areas of church music—the hymns, the organ music and the anthems by the choir—there is ample opportunity for a gradual program of education in the true nature of worship and the distinction between music which is inferior and that which is worthy of its high calling as "an help to devotion."

*   *   *

The largest and most formal musical offering of the service is, and always has been, the work of the church choir. The basic principles of choir work take their origin in the fact that the choir is a human organism. I make no distinction between a church choir and a school or college chorus. In both instances the object is not so much to prepare a series of pieces of music as to train and develop a chorus, a body of singers which has both musical proficiency and that mysterious but vital sense of artistic unity. Choirmasters are particularly prone to look no farther than the anthem for next Sunday morning. On the contrary, they should take a long range view of the year. There is a majestic rhythm in the church year, marked by the great festival seasons. This immediately suggests for the choir a series of main objectives: first, a period of basic training in the autumn, then preparation for Advent and Christmas; then the Lenten season and Easter; and finally the conclusion of the year. Through a skillful selection of larger and smaller anthems and through the excellent practice of repetition (which saves rehearsal time and allows the choir and the congregation to penetrate more deeply into some of the most beautiful anthems) it is possible to find time in the regular weekly schedule to prepare for the really large objectives at Christmas, during Lent, at Easter, and toward the end of the year. I am not suggesting for a moment that the music for Christmas or Easter usurp the Sunday morning service, as is all too often the case, leaving the minister little time for the sermon and curtailing the regular order of service in order to introduce "special music." Far better to follow the ancient practice of a special musical service, the *Abendmusiken,* or Vesper Service, in the late afternoon or evening, at which the choir performs either one large work, a cantata or oratorio, or a series of especially beautiful motets suited to the season.

The most perfect Christmas music is the homely and simple carols. There is no more touching musical and spiritual experience than a beautiful service of Christmas carols, some new, others old, but all simple and without pretension. Let there be no flashy and tricky Christmas carol arrangements. In the carols, as in American Negro spirituals, those settings and performances are most moving which are marked by artless simplicity.

In addition to an annual Christmas Carol service, Advent offers the occasion for a larger and more formal musical objective for the autumn season of the choir. Similarly, Lent and Easter provide the natural culmination of the spring season, with a possible secular concert or a Gilbert and Sullivan operetta in May. An excursion into secular music offers special opportunities for training in the basic arts of choral performance, and in that mysterious sense of corporate unity which derives from the combination of discipline and enjoyment and lies at the very heart of all good choral work.

The rehearsals of the choir, like those of any chorus, should be devoted to the basic virtues of tone quality and good diction; and the ultimate object of the whole operation of rehearsing is to penetrate into the unique character

of each piece of music so that it can be revealed in all its
beauty to the listeners. The words are the lodestar. No two
anthems must sound alike. The moods of triumphant
praise, mystical adoration, penitence, thanksgiving—each
should be plumbed to the depths in rehearsal, and recreated
in performance with such singleness of purpose that musical technique is absorbed in directness of communication.

Morley's definition of a motet in A *Plaine and Easie Introduction to Practicall Musicke* (1597) states the case
both for the practical and the spiritual areas in church
music. It sums up the multifarious details of choral technique in the precise admonition to "vowel and sing clean."
And it proclaims beyond any doubt the mysterious paradox
that what is offered to God by the artist in single-minded
devotion can be at the same time an edification to the
listener and "an help to devotion."

A Motet is properlie a song made for the church . . . This
kind of al others which are made on a ditty [text], requireth
most art, and moueth and causeth most strange effects in the
hearer . . . for it will draw the auditor (and speciallie the
skilfull auditor) into a deuout and reuerent kind of consideration of him for whose praise it was made. But . . . the matter is
now come to that state that though a song be neuer so wel
made & neuer so aptlie applied to the words, yet shal you
hardlie find singers to expresse it as it ought to be, for most of
our church men, (so they can crie louder in ye quier then their
fellowes) care for no more, whereas by the contrarie, they ought
to studie howe to vowell and sing cleane, expressing their
wordes with deuotion and passion, whereby to draw the hearer
as it were in chaines of gold by the eares to the consideration of
holie things.[19]

*   *   *

Let me speak now directly from my own experience as a
choirmaster to choirmasters. In far too many churches

there is a conflict, smoldering or fiery, between organist and choir or between organist and minister, or between all three and the congregation. How often we hear: "Too much Bach!" "The hymns are too difficult!" "Why these dreary anthems?"

In the campaign for better music in the churches, as in the schools, we are dealing, not so much with a technical problem, as with a human problem, a problem in education and in leadership. Let us assume that the organist and choirmaster is true to his conscience and dedicated to the best music. Let us assume also that some of the choir, or the minister, or some members of the congregation, or some combination of these forces, are equally dedicated to good music. The choirmaster has allies, but he is engaged in a battle against sentimental attachments to old hymn tunes and against a thoughtless and shallow assumption that church music is, after all, entertainment. What shall he do and what chance is there for success? The whole history of the reform movement in church music in the twentieth century proves that the dedicated choirmaster is fighting on the side of the angels.

I say to the musician: Don't lower your own standards, but don't set up such narrow standards that they shut out more than they take in. Don't limit yourself to one century, span them all. See as much good as you can in the music that is favored by those less educated than yourself. Be skillful and imaginative and ingenious at substituting for inferior music, something good, which is at the same time "popular." Let your choir repertory embrace the widest variety of beautiful music of all periods and sneak in gradually and persistently those pieces which are actively resisted by your opponents. Make a success, a thing of irresistible beauty, out of everything you touch. Extract the last drop of imagination, and the deepest feeling, out of every piece, whether it be the simplest unison anthem like Samuel Wesley's "Lead Me, Lord," or a motet of William Byrd. Once your choir has experienced the excitement of creating something absolutely beautiful, on which you and they have worked together, they are yours forever.

In the area of of musical standard there are two fallacies. The first is that good music is difficult and poor music is easy. It is only the lazy choirmaster who offers the excuse that his choir is not quite good enough to sing good music. Technical difficulties have nothing to do with it. Unison anthems, and the simplest part-songs are often the most beautiful and impressive church music. There is a power and beauty in simple dignity. The second fallacy is that all the music in the world can be divided into two classes, either absolutely good, or absolutely bad. The true picture is rather that at one extreme there is the very best, and at the other extreme the very worst, and in between a vast middle ground. The inescapable obligation of the choirmaster is to aim for the best, and his strategy is to proceed through the middle ground, climbing ever higher and higher, as he carries his choir, his minister and his congregation along with him.

The choirmaster must reflect and radiate his own conviction of the beauty of the music, rather than explain and argue it. Ask of your choir and congregation only tolerance and suspended judgment. Give the greatest music a chance and it will make its own way. This is the universal law of art.

The organist and choirmaster is a special kind of minister and teacher, doing a creative job in a special human situation which involves other human beings in the corporate act of worshiping God. He is working with beauty and working with people. He must know his craft, must be master of the techniques involved in his profession; but his greatest assets are not technical and professional, but human. They are common sense, tact, a sense of humor, infinite patience, dogged determination, energy, imagination, and a sense of timing. "Be ye therefore wise as serpents and harmless as doves."[20] Above all, have faith in people and in the power of music, a power which is not only communicative but regenerative.

In the words of the 38th Chapter of the Book of Job, "the morning stars sang together and all the sons of God shouted for joy."[21] Did you ever hear the morning stars singing together? This is not scientific prose but imaginative poetry. It is the most beautiful line I know, about—what? About music, about the sons of God, and an act of worship. No less than this is the mission of music in the church. The paradox is that when music is so offered up to God, like the morning stars singing together, a blessing comes back to the congregation and to the choir—to listeners and to singers.

⁂ CHAPTER IV · THE ARTS AND GOVERNMENT

INSOFAR as this book is a report on the current state of music, tangible progress can be recorded in the long campaign for government support of the arts. Public discussion of the issues increased noticeably during the last years of President Eisenhower's term, and has been further stimulated by official statements and activities during the administration of President Kennedy. The groundwork is being laid for a more positive participation of the state in the affairs of art and of artists.

The issues need clarification. There has been extravagant oratory on both sides. "Subsidy" has been depicted as a hideous hobgoblin by the opponents of government aid. "State support means state control, and official art fosters mediocrity."[1] "The distribution of money would be in the wrong hands and the wrong people would be running it."[2] "We just have no business spending one single dollar on things that are not necessary to our security."[3] One Congressman has asked: "What are the arts? . . . What various occupations are included in the arts, so that we will know what we are getting into?"[4] Another questioned at a committee hearing "if poker playing might not also be considered a performing art."[5]

The objections of congressmen and others to aid for the arts have been met by equally irrational claims on the part of its supporters; and there is a danger that the whole program may be killed by its friends. The *International Musician*, trade journal of the musicians' union (268,000 members) under the lurid title, "Plight of Music told to Millions," reported "a prolonged discussion between President Herman Kenin of the American Federation of Musicians and showman Arthur Godfrey, about the problems besetting music and musicians." This television interview reached the "inevitable conclusion that federal subsidy for the living arts is an absolute necessity if America's most highly developed art form is to survive."[6] In a statement to both Democratic and Republican platform committees in July 1960, Kenin referred to music as "our national secret weapon" and "the only universal language," and declared that it is "a sacred obligation of government . . . to succor our failing arts."[7] Nan Robertson reported in the *New York Times* that "the lot of the serious musician in America is a grubby and frustrating one and the government is doing nothing to save him from extinction."[8] The President of the National Council on the Arts in Government asserts that "the arts provide fall-out shelters for the human spirit."[9] Mrs. Helen Thompson, Executive Secretary of the American Symphony Orchestra League, argues that

. . . there must be established in the government of the United States a Department of Culture, whose secretary will serve as a member of the President's cabinet. . . . Only at cabinet level can the arts properly be served, and only at that level can the arts properly serve the government and the citizens of this nation. . . . I can think of nothing more disastrous to the arts of this nation and to our cultural image abroad than to have the arts relegated to a bureau or a subsection of some existing department of the government—any department, be it Defense, Agriculture, the Interior, or Health, Education and Welfare. Once so relegated—the arts probably would stay there forever![10]

John Kenneth Galbraith, Professor of Economics, and Russell Lynes, managing editor of *Harper's Magazine,* appeared in 1961 on the television show called "The Nation's

Future," to debate the question of federal support for the arts. Professor Galbraith championed the objective of elevating the artist to first-class citizenship through stronger representation in government.[11] The implication that artists are second-class citizens is matched by the union threat that without subsidy the American musician will become "as extinct as the dodo bird."[12] The use of catch-phrases is deplorable. What is needed is a balanced and dispassionate appraisal by a far larger segment of the public than has hitherto concerned itself with the arts.

*   *   *

The traditional American position with respect to government activity in artistic affairs is in sharp contrast to the ancient and universal patronage of the arts by governments in Europe. There the notion of state aid was inherited directly from the generous support of the arts, especially music, in the eighteenth and nineteenth centuries by sovereigns large and small. In the transition from kings and emperors to democratic governments, the transfer of the concept of responsibility in artistic affairs has worked out more naturally in Europe than in the United States.

Ralph Purcell has traced the history of patronage policies in the visual arts—architecture, painting, sculpture.[13] He recognizes three phases: the decorative, the acquisitive, and the promotional. The fact that his study is confined to the visual arts is a precise reflection of the main concern of American governments—national, state, and municipal —since the time of Washington and Jefferson. State capitals, court houses, post offices, and other government buildings led the way, followed by the commissioning of vast numbers of paintings, largely portraits and historical scenes, and finally the government acceptance of the gift of private art collections and the erection of museums like the National Gallery of Art. These acts attest the association of American government with the visual arts. However, both the Congress and the executive branch have had little experience with music or the other performing arts as an area of American life. It is natural, therefore, that government involvement should be questioned at every step.

In Europe, not only France, Italy, Great Britain, the Soviet Union, and Germany West and East, but also the small countries—the Netherlands, Belgium, Greece, Denmark, Sweden, Portugal, Austria, and Monaco—provide state support for music through direct and indirect subsidies. In West Germany the national and local governments contribute from \$59,000,000 to \$71,000,000 per year to the theater and opera.[14] Orchestras are supported in a few cases by direct subsidy, but more often through government-owned radio and television stations. Conservatories and ballet schools which were founded (many in the 1860's)[15] by royal or aristocratic patrons, continue to be supported by national or local governments. The state takes a hand in selecting the most talented students for admission to the conservatories, and their entire education is provided at government expense. Contemporary music has been generously fostered and promoted by the state, sometimes by direct payments to eminent living composers but more often through the subsidies to radio stations, which in turn (and in sharp contrast to the United States) make a specialty of contemporary music.

In the United States we have only recently begun to approach this complicated problem. Public interest is small, and the burden of propaganda is borne by various musical organizations, especially three: The American Federation of Musicians, the Council on the Arts and Government, and the National Music Council. A recent phenomenon is the appearance of strong allies in Washington. Senators Fulbright (D, Arkansas), Humphrey (D, Minnesota), and Javits (R, New York) and Representatives Kearns (R, Pennsylvania), Thompson (D, New Jersey), Lindsay (R, New York), and others have energetically sponsored bills in the Congress and kept the issue before the public in repeated speeches and articles. President Eisenhower proposed the bill for a Federal Advisory Council on the Arts in 1955 and both presidential candidates endorsed it in 1960.

It remained for President and Mrs. Kennedy to make a larger contribution to the arts than any of their predecessors throughout our entire history. Their interest spans the whole spectrum of the arts from the furnishings of the White House to the warm recognition of poets and musicians. Concerts, opera, and drama have found a physical home in the White House. Yet it is in the realm of the intangibles—the creation of a public climate of respect, appreciation, and receptiveness—that the Kennedys have made their unique contribution. A public demonstration of concern for the highest standards and an unspoken posture of gratitude for art and artists are far more powerful than campaigns of promotion. The American people sense this; they are aware and they are moved. August Heckscher, appointed by the President to the post of Consultant on the Arts, has insisted that the main objective of government is to develop and maintain the atmosphere and situations under which creativity can flourish.[16]

Something much more tangible than an atmosphere is the persistent demand, not only of the propaganda organizations, but of many citizens who are deeply concerned for the development of our culture. Government support of public education has been a basic policy since the founding of the republic. It is one of the most firmly rooted of American traditions. There is also ample precedent for government support in the area of the visual arts. It is argued, therefore, that some sort of subsidy for the performing arts would constitute, not a new and dangerous experiment, but an extension of an historic policy in American government.

Such support has already been ventured at the state and municipal level. This decentralization has validity in a vast country with varying local conditions. A Library of Congress survey of municipal and state aid reveals a general pattern of "Arts Councils," some generously, others meagerly, supported by public funds. The Arts Council has proved itself a convenient and accurate term to describe local control and direction, and the record shows that the fears of political interference or graft and of the loss of freedom by the artist are unwarranted. The state-wide program of the Arts Council of New York, staunchly supported by Governor Rockefeller, has been outstanding, and is, even at its earliest stage, an augury of success in a field new in American experience.

Support of the arts at the state and municipal level is not enough. Federal assistance and encouragement are as necessary here as in European countries where costs are shared by the national and local governments. No combination of consumer support through ticket sales, private philanthropy, and grants-in-aid from local governments can provide sufficient funds to sustain and promote the expanding role of the performing arts in American life. Leadership in this grand design should come from the federal government, if for no other reason than the fact that support for the arts is still an unpopular cause in the great majority of state legislatures and city governments. National concern, expressed at the highest level and implemented by financial support for specific projects on a matching basis, would provide the initiative for cultural progress long overdue in our practical-minded democracy. Federal assistance for science, pure and applied, is accepted as a commonplace incident in governmental activity. The world of the spirit, the humane ministrations of the arts, deserve similar support. The first steps have been taken and a foundation has been laid.

*　　*　　*

In the Eighty-seventh Congress, thirty-six bills and three joint resolutions dealing with the arts were submitted in the House; nine such bills were introduced in the Senate. The most important are three in number.[17] A bill for a Federal Advisory Council on the Arts would establish a consultative body of specialists to advise Congress and the Administration, to propose methods of encouraging private initiative in the arts, and to cooperate with existing governmental agencies to foster artistic and cultural endeavors. The National Cultural Development Act would authorize the yearly allotment of money to any state having a suitable art agency and proposing specific projects in any field in the arts. This federal aid would match state and local assistance for projects in the arts. A bill establishing the United States Arts Foundation would authorize the appropriation of $5,000,000 the first year, and $10,000,000 annually thereafter, to a United States Arts Foundation, which would consist of a director and twelve trustees, appointed by the President. These were modest proposals, but in the welter of congressional debate, amid the pressures for and against other items in the President's program, they were not enacted into law.

The legislative and executive situation vis-à-vis the arts changes month by month, and my report will be out of date before it is printed. A bill submitted to the Eighty-eighth Congress by Senator Humphrey (D, Minnesota) combines the three separate measures mentioned above, revising and clarifying the proposals. In Title I, the Federal Advisory Council on the Arts is renamed the National Council on the Arts, and is located in the Executive Office of the President, instead of the Department of Health, Education, and Welfare. Title II, "The National Arts Foundation Act of 1963" (which may be voted as an Act separate from Title I), combines the best features of the earlier National Cultural Development Act and the United States Arts Foundation Act. There is little likelihood that these or other acts will be passed by the Eighty-eighth Congress, or even be reported out of Committee by the House. The Senate has been far more receptive to the cause of the arts, but even there positive action will require far greater evidence of popular support than is now visible.

In April 1963 the President issued an Executive Order creating the President's Advisory Council on the Arts, thus bypassing temporarily the Congressional delay on Title I. August Heckscher served as Special Consultant on the Arts in the President's Office, from April 1952 to May 1963, the first such appointment ever made. Following a recommendation of Mr. Heckscher, President Kennedy announced on the Fourth of July, 1963, the award of the new Presidential Medal of Freedom to thirty-one persons in the arts, education, science, government, and public service, including three musicians, all performers. This is the first "honors list" of its kind in American history.

There is a certain irony in the fact that Congress has for some years supported a cultural exchange program administered in the State Department which in effect subsidizes musical performances by Americans abroad, but not at home. The implementation of the program for cultural exchange has been awarded by contract largely to ANTA (American National Theater and Academy), which since 1954 has acted as agent for the State Department.* Through June 1961 ANTA recommended and the State Department approved for assistance 140 cultural projects (not all in music) to 112 countries and other geographical units.[18] From both within and outside the government there has been criticism of the policy which has limited recommendation to professional groups (from symphony orchestras to individual artists and jazz combos), neglecting for the most part the large field of college and conservatory musicians. Such student organizations, when they have been able to raise their own funds to travel abroad, have proved excellent ambassadors and often have gotten closer to the people of countries visited than the professional groups moving on a tighter schedule of formal appearances.

The city of Washington is the peculiar responsibility of the Congress of the United States. An act of 1959 set aside a tract of government land in the District of Columbia for a National Cultural Center, to be financed by private contributions. The initial plans were extravagant, and the building costs have been scaled down from $75,000,000 to $30,000,000. A National Center for the Performing Arts would be a symbolic gesture in support of the local activities in symphonic and choral music and in opera—all privately supported. Of more practical assistance would be a working fund for performing projects more commensurate with the significance of the capital city as the center of the national government and the host to countless visitors from all over the world. Congress has appropriated $16,000 annually for

* In the spring of 1963 the State Department terminated its contract with ANTA and took over complete administration of the International Cultural Exchange Program, now restyled The Cultural Presentations Program. The Department has, however, retained the screening panels established by ANTA.

concerts and art programs, as compared with $824,000 in Philadelphia and $4,718,824 in New York.[19] It should be a matter of pride to assist Washingtonians in their effort to attain a measure of musical distinction comparable with that of other world capitals like London, Paris, and Rome.

Arthur J. Goldberg, as Secretary of Labor, was the chief spokesman for the administration in its arts policy. His pronouncement is the first American "state paper" on the relation of government and the arts. On December 14, 1961 he announced his settlement of a labor dispute which had threatened to cancel the Metropolitan Opera season of 1961–62, and appended a far longer document with the title "The State of the Performing Arts." This is the first comprehensive treatment of the subject by a high government official. Mr. Goldberg surveyed the field, historically and analytically, and balanced the need and the hazards of action. He made it clear that assistance to art and artists must involve a six-point partnership—the public itself, which has always been and must continue to be the chief support, private benefactors and patrons, private corporations, the labor organizations, local and state governments, and finally the federal government. His reasoned and sober conclusion is unanswerable. "We must come to accept the arts as a new community responsibility. . . . Part of this new responsibility must fall to the Federal Government, for precisely the reasons that the nation has given it a role in similar undertakings."[20]

*   *   *

A full-fledged Department of the Arts and Culture, headed by a Secretary who would be a member of the President's Cabinet, has been the traditional goal of many active friends of the arts and music. Serge Koussevitzky, conductor of the Boston Symphony Orchestra from 1924 to 1949, preached this doctrine up and down the land for a quarter of a century. It is clear from Mrs. Thompson's statement quoted earlier in this chapter that many protagonists will be satisfied with nothing short of an independent department and a cabinet secretary.

I propose that the interests of art be linked more closely with education. I would like to see education taken out of its present association with health and welfare (in the Department of Health, Education, and Welfare) and reorganized as a Department of Education and the Arts. The remaining two sections of HEW form a natural union; and the creation of the new department would relieve the heterogeneous, sprawling character of the largest of our government complexes. Parenthetically, the association of music with welfare brings to mind all too clearly the early days of the Works Progress Administration where, although much fine work was accomplished, the normal concerns of musical life were subordinated to the needs of relief and welfare.

It is significant that government support of performing groups through the State Department and ANTA has been limited to professionals and divorced from educational institutions and their performing groups. The professional world and the educational world should not be segregated. So far as government is concerned, this trend should be reversed. The best hope for the arts in America lies in exactly the opposite direction.

The Netherlands has combined education and the arts in the Ministry of Education, Arts, and Sciences; Mexico has a Ministry of Education and Fine Arts; and in Austria the affairs of the fine arts are cared for within the Ministry of Education. A similar union in the United States is natural and reasonable. It is a logical development of the historic American policy of support for public education through the schools. Education embraces more than universal elementary schooling; that was its primitive beginning. Music and art are more than subjects in a curriculum. A Department of Education and the Arts, headed by a cabinet Secretary, would confirm the union of all the arts in all their manifestations with the entire spectrum of education, and would signalize and affirm the maturity of our culture.

Music is a vast territory, embracing many different careers and many separate fields. My observation of the current campaign for federal support is that the proponents are concerned primarily with aid and assistance for only two of these fields, composition and performance. The propagandists seem more concerned with showcases and status, with what Professor Galbraith called first-class citizenship, than with the breadth and depth of the art of music in all its manifestations. Congressional hearings have been too much dominated by talk about "deplorable economic conditions" and the fear that "serious music" (opera and symphony orchestras) "cannot survive much longer in the United States without assistance from the Government."[21] Art, especially music, has been too often represented as a poorly paid entertainment industry in need of subsidy to give it a fair chance with other occupations.

A Department of Education and the Arts should be concerned with the entire sweep of musical activities, and with all the arts as part of life. More important, it would bind together in one fabric the interests of the arts and of education. The future of the art of music in the United States depends above all else on the education of the vast public, on the raising of standards, school by school, church by church, community by community. The future depends not alone on a favorable climate for composers and performers, with government support, but far more on a better standard of musical education in schools, colleges, conservatories, and in records, radio, and television. If the music that surrounds our daily life in the home, the school, and the church were of a higher standard, the composer and performer would be understood, appreciated, valued, and supported. Only by raising the general level of music in the country can the galaxy of our brightest stars be better served.

CHAPTER V · COMPOSER AND PUBLIC

THE FOUNTAINHEAD of music is the composer. Music flows through our contemporary life in gigantic streams, but the source of all these streams, the spring from which they issue, is the unique, peculiar, individual creative mind of the composer. It is not the same mind as that of the musical entrepreneur, although some composers are very good businessmen. It is not the mind of the teacher, the scholar, or the critic, though sometimes it is a mind remarkable in its philosophical and critical bent. Stravinsky, Hindemith, Copland, to name three, have all the best qualities of the art critic. Yet the mind of the composer is above all else a creative mind.

It is far beyond the scope of a single chapter to attempt a balanced and comprehensive account of the workings of creative genius in the music of the twentieth century. I shall limit myself to the impact of composer on public and public on composer. How well do composers communicate with the vast population of music lovers and music listeners? Should they communicate at all? And how receptive is the public to the composer? Public attitudes vary. There is intolerance—blind, unthinking dislike of the composer of today, just because he fails to sound like Brahms or Mozart. But more often there is a sense of bewilderment coupled with an honest, almost pathetic eagerness to understand the "new music."

Such understanding consists simply in responding to music in its own terms. What are the "own terms" of modern music? Our objective is to look at musical style in general in the twentieth century, and then at the separate styles of a few representative composers. You can say of every composer, whether Palestrina or Piston, Bach or Bartok, that he has his own style. When you come to sum up his creative work, and to identify his output with him and him alone, you say his style is characterized by this and that.

Most of the terms commonly used in music can best be understood, not by looking for a specialized technical definition, but by taking the common dictionary meaning of the term and applying it to music. Webster defines style as the "distinctive or characteristic mode of presentation, construction, or execution in any art." A composer's style is his own characteristic mode of construction and presentation of musical ideas. It is an amalgam of mixed ingredients: inheritances from the past; contemporary common practices; and individual, unique, peculiar, personal qualities.

Resisting the past, and often his contemporaries, the rebel strikes out on his own. Like Kipling's Explorer, he hears voices "behind the ranges."[1] The more conventional composer draws upon his inheritances and upon the common practices of his time. Some of the greatest composers have been, not rebels and revolutionaries, but men deeply indebted to the past, who built their work securely on foundations already laid. Bach was such a man, and Mozart. Aaron Copland wrote somewhat wistfully:

Mozart had one inestimable advantage as compared with the composers of later times: he worked within the "perfection of a common language." Without such a common language the Mozartean approach to composition and the triumphs that resulted would have been impossible. Matthew Arnold once put it this way: during such a time "you can descend into yourself and produce the best of your thought and feeling naturally, and without an overwhelming and in some degree morbid effort; for then all the people around you are more or less doing the same thing." It has been a long time since composers of the Western world have been so lucky.[2]

The listener to music may have a personal preference for convention or for revolt, based upon his own bent, his own nature. The annals of music reveal giants on both sides; and there is in the history of all the arts a magnificent rhythm, like the swinging of an enormous pendulum, between these extremes.

Inheritances from the past crowd around the contemporary composer as never before. No earlier generation has been so aware of its distant progenitors. Musicology, the study of the history of music, has expanded impressively in the last hundred years. Music is now a field of research, a learned discipline. Vast stores of actual music have been dredged up, transcribed, edited, analyzed, and performed. The majority of American composers are university-trained men who have lived during their formative years in an atmosphere of research. The composer of the twentieth century, unlike Bach or Mozart or Beethoven, knows about Dufay and Machaut, the isorhythmic motet and the virelais. We get from composers of today not only neo-classic and neo-Baroque music, but neo-Renaissance and neo-medieval music as well. The strongest inheritance as it bears upon the creative life of a composer is the music of his immediate predecessors. This inheritance may exert either a negative repellent force or a positive attraction. The conservative will accept the music of the late nineteenth and early twentieth centuries and build upon it; the rebel will reject it, leap over it to an earlier style for his models, or blaze a trail completely new and original.

No composer can avoid the impact of the work of his colleagues. At any period in the history of style there is a contemporary common practice. This suggests both a consensus and the interplay of crosscurrents. The consensus is more readily observable in retrospect; the crosscurrents are vividly apparent to contemporary observers and to the composer himself. Travelers from Woods Hole to Nantucket by the little Island steamers are familiar with a lightship anchored between Halfmoon Shoal and Norton Shoal, painted bright red and bearing on its side in enormous white letters its designation *Cross Rip*. It is so named for the crosscurrents and rip tides that surge about it. No figure of speech better describes the plight of the twentieth-century composer, unless it be those ominous words in Stravinsky's *Oedipus Rex:* "trivium, trivium"—"crossroads"![3]

To catalog even a partial list of the conflicting currents which buffet the creative musician is to understand something of the apparent chaos of twentieth-century music. First the initial revolt against romanticism; then the conflicting forces of nationalism and internationalism, and of neoclassicism and anti-neoclassicism, the back-to-Bach movement, the back-to-Mozart movement; and finally the resurrection of preclassical, Renaissance, and medieval styles. One group of composers has an exclusive interest in abstract, absolute, pure music; another exhibits an opposite interest in delineative, representative music, in ballet, opera, songs, and choral works. There is a roster of dogmatic systems: serialism, *musique concrète,* acoustical harmony, linear counterpoint, parameters, pandiatonicism, dodecaphony, and aleatoric music. There are the cults—the cult of jazz, and of folk music, the cult of dissonance, the cult of the complex versus the cult of the ultrasimple, cerebral music versus music of direct appeal, impressionism versus expressionism, and the cult of the gigantic versus the cult of the miniature. Some composers write larger and larger works with larger and larger bodies of performers, while others concentrate on the tiniest pieces with a mere handful of players. There is a passionate interest in sound for the sake of sound, from the loudest and most horrendous to mere wisps surrounded by silence—an everlasting quest for new sonorous effects as opposed to a strictly limited interest in line, pattern, and structure, quite independent of sonority. Paul Hindemith was so unconcerned about tone color that he wrote music to be played by any instruments available, identified not as violins, clarinets, bassoons, but only as the highs, the middles, and the lows. Finally, in the twentieth century (as at all other periods in the history of music), there is the interest in craftsmanship, the manipulation of musical ideas for their own sake, counterbalanced by the volcanic urge to communicate ideas, moods, emotions, and states of consciousness.

Individual composers and groups of composers espouse one or another school or cult, and many respond in turn to a series of influences. In trying to understand the music of our day we ought never to forget the dilemma of the creative artist in the midst of so great a conflict of crosscurrents. Where in that turbulent sea shall he chart his own course? What chance has he to speak with a unique individual voice, that which is his and his alone? Yet he must. In the amalgam of his style, unique personal qualities must be added to inheritances from the past and contemporary common practices.

We are too close to twentieth-century music to distinguish the permanent from the transitory, the wheat from the chaff. But I am convinced that there have been three stars of first magnitude—Stravinsky, Schönberg, and Bartok, surrounded by a whole galaxy of men nearly as important, many of them Americans. I doubt that there has been such a galaxy since the Renaissance.

*　　*　　*

Looking back over sixty years, one can distinguish a durable central core of music, with its roots in the soil of the past, and its flowers and fruit revealing a distinct new idiom of common practice. Outside the central core, there have been, are now, and always will be composers who go off on a tangent. Some, like shooting stars, burn brilliantly and then vanish. Others, more like the satellites, respond to the strong pull of gravity toward the central core, and find their permanent orbit there. Such is frequently the biographical pattern of the rebellious artist—an *enfant terrible* in his youth, later a steady, disciplined craftsman, quite conventional in his style. Honegger and Milhaud come immediately to mind as examples.

The mainstream or central core of twentieth-century music includes men as diverse as Stravinsky and Bartok, Vaughan Williams and Roussel, Martinu and Milhaud, Piston and Poulenc, Hindemith and Britten, Copland and Prokoviev. The "common practice" style of the twentieth century involves the decreased importance of melody as the nineteenth century understood it, and the increased importance of rhythm; perpetual motion, sometimes regular, sometimes highly irregular; driving energy; extremely chromatic harmony; ever more striking orchestral sonorities; and the acceptance of unresolved dissonance as a staple ingredient in all music. These differences in style, as compared with that of the nineteenth century, are not defects. The new music does not sound like Chopin or Chaminade, Brahms or Schubert. Yet this style has grown out of the soil of the past, and represents logical steps in the evolution of musical art.

Many of the old formal designs and techniques of composition have proven remarkably durable—the variations, with a continuous history from the Renaissance; the fugue and the passacaglia, with origins in the early Baroque; the classical sonata, a "grand" form today as it was in Beethoven's time; the ballet phraseology, characteristic of dances from sarabande to Stravinsky; and the imitative technique, as old as counterpoint itself.

Music constructed on these techniques of composition and manifesting these naturally evolving style characteristics should present no real difficulties to the listener who has been brought up through Brahms, Wagner, and Debussy to the threshold of the twentieth century. Even *Sacre du Printemps,* whose first performance in 1913 created a typical French *scandale,* now appears as a logical, though harsh and drastic, development in a continuous straight line from the practices of the nineteenth century. Pierre Lalo was not correct when he wrote:

The cult of the wrong note has never been practiced with such zeal and persistence as in this score; from the first measure to the last whatever the note you expect, it is never that one which comes, but the one next to it; whatever chord may seem to be involved by a preceding chord, it is always another that follows.[4]

I find the mainstream of twentieth-century music very beautiful. I make no distinction in the order of aesthetic value between this music and that of the romantic period, the classic, the Baroque or any other in recorded history. I suggest that the doubting reader pick from the vast range of twentieth-century music three Third Symphonies, all American—those of Roy Harris (1939), Walter Piston (1947), and Aaron Copland (1946)—and listen with uninterrupted attention to these recordings a dozen times over a period of a month. So might he observe the variety, the richness, and the beauty of three characteristic items out of the durable tradition of symphonic literature.

*　　*　　*

In the history of art there are always the explorers. There are groups of these tangential personalities now. It is impossible to predict how permanent their work is, whether it will return to the mainstream or perhaps deflect into a new course; but it behooves us to pay attention to them. The composers of electronic music are the most recent and the most experimental. The centers of this development are certain European radio stations, or radio laboratories, notably at Cologne and Milan. The chief composers are the German Karlheinz Stockhausen, the French Pierre Boulez, and the Italian Luciano Berio. The first experimental laboratory in the United States is an electronic music center at Columbia University, under the joint control of Columbia and Princeton, established by a five-year grant of $175,000 from the Rockefeller Foundation, and directed by Milton Babbitt, Otto Leuning, and Paul Ussachevsky.

Electronic music is a creature of the new technology. So scientific have we become that the beautiful and wonderful world of flutes, violins, organs, trumpets, and lutes has been reduced to the cold precision of mathematical formulas. "Any musical instrument is essentially a data generator and/or processor."⁵ Thus the electronic composer bypasses the normal instruments and composes at his laboratory, explaining that "precise frequency control is provided by the electronic oscillator, control of temporal duration is provided by the measurement of tape length, loudness is controlled by electronic amplification of the individual sound, and spectrum is determined by the particular combination of oscillators employed to produce the individual sound."⁶

There are three sources of sound in electronic music: purely electronic sounds produced by coded instructions in the form of holes punched on a paper roll; the sounds of conventional instruments recorded on tape and then manipulated and distorted—screeching, thudding, whistling, in horrendous volume or breathless pianissimo, and at speeds faster or slower and pitches higher or lower than the original; and sounds of nature—for example, spoken words rendered strange by elongating the vowels or consonants or playing the tape at an excessive speed.

Three important techniques are involved in producing the final sound track: *filtering*—taking out the "highs" or the "lows," and so creating new timbres; *mixing*—working out diverse combinations of sound on a "patch board," roughly comparable to drawing stops on an organ; and *splicing*—fitting together several magnetic tapes.

Electronic music is performed or reproduced only through the medium of the sound track, which is amplified and distributed through a single loud-speaker or a whole battery of speakers, scattered through a hall—backstage, main floor, and balconies—or out-of-doors in the trees. The manipulator of the dials at a performance may alter the quality, but he has an obligation to respect the instructions of the composer.

The number of sound effects available to the composer through electronic means approaches infinity. For the ears of the listener there are potential sensations of sonority surpassing his wildest dreams. I have been amazed and fascinated by the extremely high and extremely low pitch levels, exceeding those of any conventional instruments.

Some listeners reject the new music altogether: "This is not music; it's only noise." But certainly it is sound, and certainly the men who put it together are musicians; according to their word, it is music—the music of the future. Whatever else be said, it remains the most unnatural, the most sophisticated, and the most completely revolutionary way of producing music. It may be destined for years of experimentation, development, and refinement; yet it will never completely supplant singing and playing.

How, then, shall the listener evaluate electronic music?

Throughout the history of the art from the most primitive times to the present, certain characteristic elements have constituted what we call music. These elements are melody and rhythm or motion. Music is sound organized in the dimension of time. Look at these sounds vertically and we call the results *harmony;* so defined, harmony may be either consonant and euphonious and pleasant, or it may be dissonant and discordant. Look at a number of strands of melody going on at the same time, and we call it *counterpoint.* Look at the whole fabric of sound, the disposition of the interwoven threads, and we call it the *texture* of music. Look at the shape and pattern of the whole series of sounds in time, and we call it the *form* of music. Listen to the sheer sound of music—the orchestral effects, the blend of an *a cappella* choir in a stone church, or a hundred other varieties—and we call it the element of *sonority.*

Which of these basic elements exist in electronic works? Not melody, not rhythm, not harmony, not counterpoint, not texture, and not form as understood today. There is only one valid element of music in these pieces—the sound itself. This is one of the most important factors. The whole history of music is a history of sonority, from the chanting of the monks in a medieval abbey to the fantastically varied sonorities of the *Sacre du Printemps;* from the sonorous effect, the *matière sonore,* of a Mozart symphony to that of a jazz combo. I am fascinated by sonority. Much of the history of nineteenth- and twentieth-century music is the history of the exploration and discovery of new sonorities—by Berlioz, Rimsky-Korsakov, Richard Strauss, Mahler, Debussy, Ravel, Stravinsky, Aaron Copland.

The sonorities available to the electronic composer are of another order. Small wonder that composers are excited by the apparently endless possibilities of breaking the barriers which bound and limit conventional instruments! It seems strange, however, that up to now, all the other basic elements of music are, so far as I can discover from listening, entirely absent in electronic compositions. No melody, no harmony, no rhythm, no form—only sonority. This is something new in the history of music. There has always been, not only sound, but sounds organized in motion, in time, in rhythm; a linear component called melody; a number of linear components called counterpoint; and a vertical component called harmony. Musical art has always involved an order. Indeed, art is order, form, structure, and logic. Possibly the new music contains aspects of texture, of form, even of rhythm, but so far I have been unable to detect them. In time the more traditional elements of musical art, now absent, will make their way into the new scores. Then we shall have an art form which would be a natural development along the great central current of musical history.

Turning back from the most extreme radicals, we encounter the composers who, though they experiment with electronic music, also work with conventional instruments and voices. Their style involves some connection with the past, notably the serial technique of Schönberg, Berg, and Webern, as well as the rhythmic, metallic, percussive idiom of Stravinsky. Their melodic style is highly disjunct, angular, and pulverized. The harmony is dissonant. There is a trace of counterpoint and a slight feeling of motion and rhythm. If there is any formal organization, it is a secret.

Why is the form of this music so difficult to follow? Because the repetitions in the music are not distinguishable. Repetition is the *sine qua non* for understanding the form of sounds in time. Sir Donald Tovey said that the listener should approach a piece of music as one "who knows nothing beforehand, but hears and remembers everything."[7] But you cannot remember this music; there is nothing for the ear or the mind or the memory to grasp and retain!

It is not the dissonance nor the weird sound effects that

trouble me; it is the apparent formlessness, the lack of order. The new sounds and rhythms are exciting, dramatic, clean, and bracing—like a bitter wind on a clear zero day. Life is not all consonance and euphony; dissonance is life, or a part of it. So I find dissonance true. But the absence of a deliberate movement forward toward some objective or point of arrival, the absence of any discernible pattern or order—these qualities baffle me.

Since the new music avoids the durable conventional forms (concerto, sonata, symphony, fugue, variations), and since the music is rarely descriptive or delineative ("Till Eulenspiegel," "Daphnis et Chloé"), new titles must be invented. The attempt to ascribe some formal design— new and utterly unconventional—to the works of the avant-garde can be traced in their choice of titles. Some sense of groping toward a new world of patterns is evident if one compares the new titles with some of the older names of small pieces. For Adagio, Ballade, Capriccio, Étude, Impromptu, Intermezzo, Prelude, Scherzo, read:

Antiphony One	Motus-colorus
Apparitions	Music in Two Dimensions
Circles	Perspectives
Contacts	Polyphony
Cross cross	Progressions in Tempo
Cycle	Quantities
Doubles	Sequence
Folio	Spectra
Incantations	Structures
Interpolations	Tempo

"566 to Henry Flynt"

The newest nonelectronic music has brought to the fore experiments in notation and in improvisation. Notation is the shorthand by which the composer indicates to the performer what to play and how to play it. It has always been, and it remains, a most inexact, unscientific science. The music farthest on the radical left has had to develop a new notation. The scores consist of large pieces of cardboard covered with squares, circles, and code designs. On the stage at a performance these cardboards require from two to four music stands, and they are sometimes replaced by a great stretch of folded paper running halfway around the stage. The cardboards can be shuffled at will. It is a weird sight. The performer is king. He improvises his part from the cryptic notational directions on the cardboards. But here, at this very point, is a historical constant in the transaction. Improvisation is not new. It is as old as—far older than—the *basso continuo* practice of the seventeenth century. In this technique the harpsichord player in a piece of concerted music had before him on the music rack only a bass part, nothing more, with or without figures indicating the outlines of the harmonies. From the bass part the player improvised a right hand part and filled in the inner parts. There was no one right way to do it, and no two realizations were alike. There was the widest opportunity for originality, inventiveness, and good taste—in short, a fine art of improvisation. Similarly, singers with a simple line like the aria which is known as Handel's "Largo," invented their own coloratura, and violinists in a Corelli "Adagio" embellished their part with elaborate "colorations."

If improvisation is as old as the Baroque, and older, it is as new as modern jazz, where 98 percent of the musical performance is improvised on the barest skeleton of melody and bass. Improvisation by the performer and a free and flexible system of notation are characteristics of the new music. The pendulum will undoubtedly swing back toward a more exact notation and a less improvisatory performance, as it did between the seventeenth and the nineteenth centuries. Art moves in a rhythm of great cycles from one extreme to the other.

*   *   *

The serial technique or twelve-tone system of Schönberg, Berg, and Webern has presented great difficulties for the ordinary listener in comparison with music of the mainstream or central core. Schönberg and his two eminent disciples have long been recognized as among the truly great figures of the century, yet it is only in the last decade that there has begun to be either popular understanding or a considerable body of professional followers.

The main principles of this craft of composition appear to be didactic, mathematical, and inflexible. Each individual work is based on a series of notes, a tone-row, which involves a succession of all twelve chromatic tones in the scale, the succession, the time values, and the phraseology determined by the composer. This tone-row or series remains unchanged through the piece, which consists therefore of a series of restatements. The original tone-row may be inverted; or it may be played backward in retrograde form; or the retrograde may itself be inverted. Furthermore, any one of these four patterns may be transposed to any step of the chromatic scale, so that there are actually twelve times four, or forty-eight, possible modifications of the basic tone-row. The tone-row may be interpreted horizontally, as melody, or vertically (in whole or in part) as harmony. This would appear to be music for the eye and the brain, not for the ear. Amid the tangled web of microscopic detail, the order provided by the system cannot be aurally perceived. Yet this is irrelevant. There have been periods in the past when the actual constructive technique of music itself was highly complicated.

Bach and many others have used the technique of inversion and retrograde in complicated patterns which are clear to the eye in the score but which the ear cannot possibly follow. Nonetheless, this music of the past has held a fascination for the intellectual performer, the sensitive listener, and for other composers. Whether Bach or Okeghem or Webern, it is the musical coherence and emotional fidelity that determines the aesthetic and communicative power.

Even before the formulation of the principles of composition with twelve tones a new style appeared in Viennese music, an aural style as easily grasped by the ear as the diagrammatic structure is clear to the eye. This style is melodic and contrapuntal, but the melodies are sharply angular and highly chromatic. Since the twelve chromatic tones are equal, there is no pull of gravity toward a tonal center. The piece is not in C major, or A-flat major, or B minor; it is atonal. The system razed what had taken centuries to build; it destroyed the analytical language of the tonal system and eliminated such terms as dominant, tonic, and key—which had become household words. Most twelve-tone music is chamber music, music for small combinations rather than for large orchestras or choruses. It is a literature of miniatures; the total output of Webern has been collected on four discs, eight sides of long-playing recordings. During the fifties and early sixties many young composers have joined this cult of the miniature, writing pieces which are mostly silence, with a minimum of notes—imitating, after twenty years, Webern's style without Webern's gifts.

The serial technique of composition is now undeniably a branch of twentieth-century common practice. Few young composers can afford to neglect its disciplines. It used to be fashionable and plausible to rationalize an antithetical polarity separating the categories of Stravinsky and Schönberg; but in the last decade Stravinsky has himself assimilated many aspects of the serial technique. Though the system appears coldly calculated and mathematical, the spirit of the music remains paradoxically true to its Viennese sources —warm, romantic, always sensitive. The amateur listener understands this, and is, in ever-increasing numbers, receptive to its beauties.

Finally, the last decade has seen the rise of a new romanticism, which, though its roots are in the grand, flamboyant, dramatic style of the nineteenth century, is tightly controlled through formal logic. The universals of the twentieth century are all present—dissonance, complexity, the linear view, the brutal sonorities. At the same time, neoclassicism and serialism, Stravinsky and Schönberg, have been assimilated and reconciled, and the strong individual voice of the composer himself has begun to emerge, speaking to the heart as well as the mind. Of the younger generation of Americans, I venture to classify Elliott Carter and Leon Kirchner among such voices— heralds of a return to the "grand style."

*   *   *

Paul Fromm, President of the Fromm Music Foundation, foremost in its discriminating assistance to contemporary composers, has referred to the young professional composers as the loneliest men in contemporary music. "Although they are aware of everything that really is contemporary, they have no one with whom to share this awareness. Their chances of entry into public musical life have been barred by the insurmountable barrier of their own originality and the hostility of individuals and institutions who deny the public anything that cannot be standardized."[8] This is a harsh judgment, which puts the blame on the public and on the musical organizations.

I distinguish two opposite attitudes toward the public on the part of the composers. One of the men deeply involved in writing serial technique and electronic music, Professor Milton Babbitt of Princeton, has compared himself to his colleagues in the physics laboratory, men who are working in pure science. He points out that they talk a language which the public cannot understand. If the pure scientist has no need to address an audience larger than his fellow scientists, why should the composer undertake to communicate with any listeners beyond his own colleagues who understand him and his music?[9] At the other pole, Aaron Copland, in addressing his Charles Eliot Norton lectures at Harvard to "the gifted listener," "the nonmusician," "the listener who intends to retain his amateur status," said: "It is the thought of just such a listener that excites the composer in me."[10]

The creative artist must find his own position between these extremes, and the public must respect the composer's right to address whom he pleases—the millions, as Beethoven did in the *Ninth Symphony* ("Seid umschlungen, Millionen") or the narrow circle of his fellow specialists.

Soviet music offers an example of music addressed to the widest possible audience. Its ultra-simplicity, the soul-stirring ardor of its marches, its ebullient optimism are calculated to appeal to the masses at home and abroad. Shostakovich said, "Music is a means of unifying broad masses of people. I am a Soviet composer and I see our epoch as something heroic, spirited, and joyous. Good music lifts and heartens, and lightens people for work and effort."[11] The calculated style of party-line music rejects nearly all the main qualities of the twentieth century and harks back to the idiom of Beethoven and German romanticism, overlaid with a few "wrong notes" and peppered with out-of-place sharps and flats. At mid-century it is old-fashioned and banal.

By contrast, Bela Bartok, though he never made a statement about communication, has since his death in 1945 been discovered by an ever-widening circle of listeners. Without compromise, and embracing all the acerbities of twentieth-century style, he has drawn the common people to him. His star continues to rise, not only among the professionals, but among men everywhere.

Practical problems in the area of musical logistics have contributed to the scarcity of performances of new music. The extreme difficulty of the scores requires more rehearsals than anybody can pay for. Luciano Berio asked for two complete free days of continuous rehearsing for a New York performance of his "Circles." Dr. Karl Geiringer reports that many years ago he attended ten public rehearsals (in addition to an earlier series of private rehearsals) for the Berlin performance of a new work by Schönberg.

Bold prophets among the avant-garde have predicted that the modern symphony orchestra, which has been the most characteristic single feature of musical life since Beethoven, is doomed by the new music. Present rehearsal schedules do not allow enough rehearsal time. Most twelve-tone composers from the start have ignored the large orchestra; their style belongs to elite chamber groups. Electronic music supersedes the orchestra, and aleatoric music is possible only with a few players who can "practice" improvising together. A new relation between composer and performer is emerging in the composer-performer workshop, where young specialists (such as the Lenox Quartet, Adele Addison, Bethany Beardslee, the groups of Fromm Players) work in closest contact with the creative artist. All these factors contribute to a narrowing of the public for new music. The dilemma of our day is that, at just the moment in history when the media of mass communication are available for the largest audience, the art forms address an ever smaller and more elite clientele.

*　　*　　*

The thoughtful and concerned amateur will ask one more question about contemporary music. Paul Tillich has spoken of what he calls the prophetic mission of art, the obligation to pass judgment on current reality. He is referring (in the visual arts) to those paintings which clearly have a message. Is there such music in the twentieth century? Oliver Wendell Holmes, Jr., in an 1884 Memorial Day address to the Grand Army of the Republic at Keene, New Hampshire, said: "it is required of a man that he should share the passion and action of his time at peril of being judged not to have lived."[12] Beethoven shared the passion and action of his time and symbolized his age, the epoch of the French Revolution, the classic conflict between tyranny and freedom. Berlioz and Wagner represented the Romantic century; Bach and Handel the Baroque. Whose music will be symbol and emblem of the twentieth century?

For the listener there are two possible approaches to contemporary music: the emotional and the analytical. My plea is for a less precipitate emotional reaction and for a more deliberate analytical approach. In Webster's words, defining "style," we can observe the "distinctive or characteristic mode of presentation, construction, or execution"[13] in a piece of new music. We can see which elements are stressed, which are neglected or downgraded, what is new, what is old or an adaptation of the old. Then and only then can we form a balanced judgment.

If we dare call ourselves music lovers, we cannot escape our responsibility toward new music. Serge Koussevitzky once said, "If we do not support the new, there will soon be no old."[14] Throughout his entire life, from his early days in Russia through his quarter of a century with the Boston Symphony Orchestra, Koussevitzky felt it was his mission as a performer to serve the living composer, to stand before the public as a champion of music new and old, popular and unpopular, easy to understand and tough to grasp hold of. His successor, Charles Munch, in a letter to one of his audience, stated the case with characteristic reasonableness:

> You reproach me for playing too much contemporary music, and I understand your point of view since you come to concerts for amusement or distraction or perhaps for consolation—surely for pleasure. But we are asking you to do something, to participate actively in an exchange between performer and public when we want you to listen to something new, something difficult to understand, even difficult to listen to especially at first encounter.
> It is our duty to the young to give them the opportunity to be heard. Music written on paper must be realized and considered. The painter's work or the sculptor's work, when completed, exists for all to see. Music to exist must be played and who is to play it if we do not? I tell you frankly that it would be easier for us to play only older music just as it would be easier for you as a listener, but if we impose this restriction on ourselves, we should be abandoning our obligation to history.[15]

It is a strange fact in the history of art that never until the twentieth century has there been such an exclusive interest in the music of the past, as opposed to the music of the contemporary composer. Throughout the Renaissance, the Baroque, and right on through Haydn, Mozart and Beethoven, performers paid little attention to the music of the past and concentrated on the music of their own day because their patrons and audiences were eager to hear the latest thing.

The modern army of listeners has not yet manifested a like curiosity about the new and a tolerance of the difficult, the tough, and the experimental. The problems arising from the new grammar and syntax of music can be cleared up for the listener through familiarity, and if there were more recordings of contemporary music our task would be easier. To understand the music of our day, the listener must bend every effort to penetrate below the surface of the notes, the dissonances, the cerebral structures, and the apparent confusion. He must give himself to an earnest search for the beauties that are without doubt there, as they have been in musical art for over a thousand years. The serious listener will approach the music of his contemporaries with curiosity, tolerance, imagination, and above all perseverence. There is a world of beauty in the new music. *Take what belongs to you,* but welcome the experimental and the challenging. "Prove all things, hold fast that which is good."[16]

✸ CHAPTER VI · THE PERFORMER

THE MUSICAL transaction is unique in the creative world. It involves both composer and performer. A painting, a cathedral, a statue, a poem, or a novel needs no re-creator to come between the creator and the observer. Only the drama and the dance resemble music in demanding a performance, and even the drama comes to life in a silent reading without action.

Music may be said to exist when it consists of no more than black notes on white paper. The notes are the composition; they are all the composer left to us, and all he could leave. Yet, in a very real sense, the composer's score is no more than a kind of musical shorthand, a guide to the performer. No two performances can possibly be alike in all details; each is a re-creation. There is no such thing as the one perfect performance. We only try to come as close to it as we can, in our finite fallibility.

The performer is not the equal of the composer, in a hierarchy of absolute values, but he is equally indispensable. The listener, for whom beyond all argument the score was written, confronts it only through the interpreter. Performance is a high calling. It is no wonder that the young person considering a career in music thinks first of performance. To be a musician is to be a performer.

In the mysterious economy of the talents, the gift to perform, to sing and to play, has been scattered with incredible prodigality over the human race. In relative terms, composers are few, performers legion. If one counts only the native gift of a pleasing and powerful voice, or a lightning dexterity of the fingers, nature has lavished her bounty with reckless abandon.

Here is the crux of the problem of careers in music. I should like to approach this problem, not as a statistical abstraction, but in the most personal and intimate terms, for it touches the very lives of human beings. It embraces golden opportunities, fabulous successes, and the bitterest personal tragedies. The grim realities of success and failure have rarely been faced either by musicians or by those eager to champion the art of music and to help young people.

Whether, as in the gospel parable,[1] there be ten talents, or five, or one has been the preoccupation of musicians and public to an exaggerated degree. There has been too much reliance on types of mechanical testing and on the contest system to determine in any given case the number and nature of the talents. There has been a blind faith that the ten-talent man could be positively identified by a battery of tests or by the ordeal of competition, and that once located, he would, *ipso facto,* soar to the zenith as an artist.

We hear a great deal about "the gifted child." Ominous words! They conjure up the individual microcosm, the body and the soul, the human being which is the ultimate source of the entire art of music in all its manifestations—composer, performer, scholar, professional, amateur. The gifted child may turn out to be a twentieth-century Beethoven or the most brilliant pianist of his generation. The alternative is equally clear: he may attain neither of these ends, nor any other frame or status. The high ratio of failure to success is tragic, and the tragedies are personal, each one peculiar and solitary.

The vast reservoir which feeds these two streams of success and failure is simply the human reservoir of a deep personal love of music, plus some gift for it. The gift may be in singing or playing or composing. It often manifests itself very early. Parents are amazed. The earliest teachers feel that they have in their hands something precious, a gifted child, possibly a Mozart. The boy or girl feels irresistibly drawn to music. He says, "That is the life for me; I can't be happy anywhere else." Orpheus and Apollo and Saint Cecilia beckon him on to a rich and happy life in music.

But where? And how? My own observation is that nine times out of ten—no, ninety-nine times out of a hundred— the family and the teacher closest to the young prodigy are aware of only two milestones on the long, long road to success: the situation they are now in, where talent has clearly manifested itself at an early age; and the ultimate goal, the stage of the Metropolitan Opera House, or the conductor's box in front of the New York Philharmonic Orchestra, or the piano bench beside the keyboard of a ten-foot concert grand, with the top up and the floodlights concentrated on the single figure in the center of the stage.

We must face the fact that not every talented child can sing at the Metropolitan, or play in Carnegie Hall, or conduct a great orchestra, or compose a *Ninth Symphony*. There are far too many gifted children. Yet these positions in the spotlight are the goals, conscious or unconscious, of thousands and thousands of children and their parents and their teachers. Conservatories and colleges are full of young men and young women who cherish the same vision of the future. The fading of that dream, sometimes gradual, sometimes shattered at one stroke, is one of the catastrophes of life.

It is my belief that there are factors in the present organization of the musical world which exaggerate the evils of the situation and which ought to be eradicated. And it is my belief that there are now for the first time a large number of alternative careers in music which can offer just as happy a life for the gifted.

*   *   *

It is the experience of every musician, I suppose, to be asked to listen to a young pianist or violinist or flute player or singer and to be faced with those simple, terrifying questions: "Does my child have talent? Should he go into music?" Of course there is talent there—one talent, or five, or ten—but the real question is what does the parent or teacher mean by "going into music."

Let us assume that the talented child and his parents decide that he shall "go into music." In elementary and secondary school he continues his studies in singing or playing with a good or not-so-good teacher, a wise or not-so-wise mentor and guide. Then comes the choice between college and conservatory; if he is a brilliant performer he will undoubtedly choose the conservatory, though some young people looking forward to careers as performing artists feel that a liberal college education is a wise thing and find a way to continue professional study along with college work.

By the age of eighteen to twenty many of the young geniuses have faded out and become ordinary citizens, playing in the college or conservatory orchestra or singing in the choir or taking part in operatic productions, but no longer aiming for the bright lights of the concert stage. But even at this age there remain thousands of young people beckoned on by the lure and the glamour of a virtuoso career. Already in college or conservatory there are prizes and awards, made on the basis of competition, with the unquestioned assumption that competition will reveal the *best* pianist or the *most* gifted singer or the *most* promising composer.

If the brilliant young performer—and there are thousands the country over—remains at the top through conservatory or college, then comes the decade of the twenties —twenty-one to thirty—and here he enters the world of the more glittering prizes. These prizes, like those in college and conservatory, are awarded to Mr. A who is judged to be positively better than Mr. B, and to Miss X who is, by some incontrovertible standard of measurement, significantly more gifted than Miss Y.

The contest business has grown rapidly in the last ten years. I view it with great alarm. There are contests in all fields of music, but chiefly in solo performance, more rarely in composition or conducting. Americans have begun to win contests in Brussels and in Moscow as well as in New York, and have returned home to ticker tape parades. Rich prizes for young artists are awarded on both sides of the Atlantic by foundations, municipalities, committees, corporations, and patrons, princely and common. All are honestly trying to do something for art. There is the Tchaikovsky Prize, the Paderewski Prize, the Mitropoulos Prize, and the Queen Elizabeth of Belgium Prizes, the Naumburg and the Leventritt and the Morgenstern competitions, the Rome International Competition in Conducting, and many, many more. One of the most recently established is the Van Cliburn Quadrennial International Piano Competition at Fort Worth, Texas. In 1962 there were 86 contestants, 37 foreign and 49 American; and the distinguished board of judges included six Americans and five foreign virtuosi.[2]

The Metropolitan Opera auditions have built up a vast organization of regional contests with an elaborate apparatus of publicity—Junior League sponsorship, prominent judges, and public acclaim for the winner. Such a national network of auditions involves at every stage the elimination of the second best, in an ever-narrowing circle, up to the semi-finals—and on to the summit, where the victor is proclaimed the best in the whole country and awarded a contract at the Metropolitan.

In the field of instrumental performance, the winner of one of the most respected competitions "will receive a cash

award of $5,000, a two-year management contract, . . . a
fully subsidized European and American concert tour prior
to an appearance with the New York Philharmonic during a
special week of non-subscription concerts, a solo recital in
New York City, and a recording for Columbia Records."[3]
This array of prizes goes to a single man, the winner. What
happens to the competitors who were eliminated along the
way? What happens to the very next man, the runner-up,
who must have been exceptionally fine, but who was adjudged by a jury of experts somehow inferior to his colleague?

The apparatus of contests, prizes, front-page publicity for
the winners, and never a mention of the losers, pervades
our musical life. In addition to state and regional contests
at the secondary level, there are more glamorous contests.

The eight finalists chosen to participate in the "Musical
Talent in Our Schools" broadcasts, sponsored jointly by the
New York Times and radio station WQXR, will be heard in
four weekly programs.

The young musicians were selected by auditions from more
than 150 competing students from public, private and parochial
high schols of the metropolitan area. After preliminary auditions, students with exceptional ability were heard in the finals
by a panel of judges comprising Artur Rubinstein, Rudolf
Serkin, Isaac Stern, Leonard Rose and Abram Chasins.

Mr. Chasins, music director of WQXR, is in charge of the
"Musical Talent in Our Schools" project, which is now in its
eleventh season. The performers will be introduced and interviewed by Mr. Chasins in the Broadcasts.[4]

Imagine the scene: eight young finalists, interviewed
over radio and television and playing in an atmosphere electric with the presence of world-famous artists. Undoubtedly
everyone was moved by the most sincere desire to help young
musicians, but did they ever try to estimate the effect of this

sort of summitry on a sixteen-year-old winner and, more important, on the sixteen-year-old losers?

Three things are wrong with our highly publicized programs for the assistance of talented musicians and our reliance on contests as the operating basis for the awards:

the winner gets too much;

the loser suffers a drastic curtailment of opportunities;

the entire philosophy of the contest belongs to the world of sports rather than to the world of art.

The winner, proclaimed with the overemphasis so characteristic of modern techniques of promotion and advertising, is catapulted into the star system, which is another deplorable characteristic of American concert life and the American operatic stage. Unlike the prize fighter, the winner of a musical contest seldom if ever has to defend his title. In the world of art defeated contestants never get a chance to challenge the winner again.

The losers, many of them highly gifted, confront the sum of human misfortune. The dreams of years of preparation come shattering down about their heads. Without the prestige and the seal of the contest winner, concert managers refuse to book a young singer or player, and promising careers come to an abrupt end.

The teacher who gives extravagant encouragement to a talented boy or girl of ten and the doting parents of such a gifted child should contemplate the risks of failure, or what is adjudged failure, in the cruel world of musical competition. The element of chance is more often than not the supreme arbiter. The winner happened to be in the right place at the right time, and he had undoubted nerve, drive, flair, and the innate ability to seize the advantage. The losers, in far too many competitions, were plain unlucky.

Turning to the underlying philosophy, the contest in art is an importation from the world of games and sports, never quite comfortable in its new environment. The contests of the Meistersingers in the Middle Ages emulated the athletic and chivalrous tournaments of that far-off time, with their elaborate trappings of protocol, their banners, their splendor, their princely court, their beautiful ladies—the publicity apparatus of that day.

In Wagner's re-creation of those classical contests in *Die Meistersinger,* Beckmesser personifies one of the inevitable defects of the contest in art. Whether a thousand years ago or today a competition cannot be set up without regulations and the paraphernalia of the rule book. This is a fundamental misunderstanding of the nature of art. To award so many points for this and so many points for that implies a compartmentalization of performance in art which is not realistic. I have served on juries for vocal contests at which I was asked to observe strictly the allotment of percentages for breath control, head resonance, *bel canto,* intonation, diction, dramatic power, poise, personality, and projection. I was asked to add them all up and award the prize to the contestant who had the highest score, even though his nearest rival was one point below. I confess I found myself going back over the separate areas of evaluation and making alterations in the points awarded until I could get the total "to come out right," because you cannot arbitrarily divide the whole man, the true artist, into a series of fractions at 10 percent apiece. In *Die Meistersinger,* Walther won the hand of Eva because of all the judges, only Beckmesser insisted on the rules, and he was a fool.

I have sat on panels where the judges found it impossible to agree. Evaluation in art is a highly subjective business. Judges are not machines but personalities. Yet we had to agree; so the winner became winner, not from any absolute scientific demonstration of his superiority but as a result of compromises between the judges. This is a pretty unstable and unreliable method of picking a first prize, and it renders all the more heartbreaking those failures who go away from the competition either rebellious or crushed by a sense of their own inadequacies.

I am convinced that contests do more harm than good. Yet they are here to stay, and the most we can hope for is some downgrading of their tyranny over the professional world of playing and singing. The contest system and the star system are inextricably woven together, and both are wrong. If we could get away from the star system in opera and on the concert stage we would do away largely with the abuses and the evils of the contests, because there would be more room for more careers for more artists.

The controlling fact is that there are far too many gifted children ever to become top-ranking performers in the presently organized concert or operatic world. To aim for the summit is perfectly natural for the ardent youth, but it is disastrously unrealistic.

*　*　*

The critical moment for the young artist comes in the twenties, at the conclusion of his professional training. How and where shall he take the next step? His American training is now, in mid-century, as good as he could obtain in Europe, possibly better. Young singers go abroad not so much to study as to find jobs; and not a few young Americans have had successful careers in the opera houses of small German cities, singing a large repertory of roles, leading and secondary, and enjoying full-time employment.

In the United States, the most encouraging development in recent times has been the spread of local opera companies and opera workshops which stress the living dramatic aspects of opera as well as its vocal phase. The decentralization of opera offers the only hope for any extensive utilization of the large number of qualified young singers. Even half a dozen seasons in addition to the Metropolitan, like those at Chicago and San Francisco, hardly make a dent on the supply of good singers, especially since these other opera companies employ many of the same stars as the Metropolitan. Yet a public for opera exists in small cities and college towns throughout the country. There is no reason why the United States should not have what Europe has had for generations—local opera companies with resident singers, orchestras, and staff.

There is a growing movement for opera with American subjects, still in its infancy but slowly gathering momentum. This is interesting and promising and should attract native composers to a field which they have mainly neglected, for want of any opportunity for performances.

The continuous debate about opera in English is a token of widespread interest. On the one side is the example of the local companies in Germany, Italy, and Russia, where all operas, no matter what their original language, are performed in the native tongue. On the other side is the recognized difficulty of English translation, and the bad example of most of the current translations, where ridiculous and inferior texts do violence to the inherent accent of the melodic phrase, the very life of the music. A further argument against translation is that poor diction often renders the English quite as unintelligible as the original language.

Local companies need not espouse either horn of the dilemma, though some will choose to cast their lot with the strong proponents of vernacular opera. A broad repertory and a flexible language policy would seem to be the best strategy. Special fields like chamber opera, television opera and the whole range of comic opera, from Italian *buffa* to

Gilbert and Sullivan, are especially suited to young singers and small companies. A local or regional opera troupe which offered a few examples of grand opera, mixed with ingredients from the varied literature outside grand opera, should make an attractive season.

A small company in Raleigh, North Carolina, has taken the name Grass Roots Opera. There could be no more appropriate symbol to describe the enormous uncultivated field for opera in the United States. The initiative must come from the local communities, here and there, one by one. Imagination, energy, persistence, patience, and determination on the part of all those with any interest in the development of opera as one aspect of the cultural revival in the United States are the essentials. The nonessentials are federal aid and foundation support, though both might help to launch the enterprise. The Ford Foundation has inaugurated a small project under which it guarantees to pay the salaries of a limited number of young singers who are engaged by the directors of small opera companies. Matching grants to local arts councils from federal or state funds might stimulate municipal governments to supplement the historic American policy of support of public schools with a parallel support of cultural projects such as opera. However, the primary responsibility for the future of opera in America rests, not in New York or Washington, and surely not with the Metropolitan, but in an awakening concern both for opera itself and for the careers of young American singers—centered in small cities and regional groups throughout the country.

Turning to the recital stage, the best hope for young singers is to cultivate a specialty, a bit off the beaten track, and to do it superlatively well—Moussorgsky, Charles Ives, Purcell, Monteverdi, the Baroque, or Latin American songs. There is a growing appreciation of the literature of the solo song from the Middle Ages to Schönberg and Boulez, and the imaginative young singer will make the most of these uncultivated fields instead of seeking to emulate the stereotype programs of many of the stars who travel the professional recital circuit.

There has been a recent growth of small professional choirs such as the Robert Shaw Chorale, the Roger Wagner Chorale, and the Margaret Hillis Choir. Many of the singers are potential soloists, and all of them are so expert as choral singers that the operations of the Chorales take place in a realm altogether beyond that of most choral organizations. During considerable periods of the year, singing in the Chorale is a full-time job for its members, whereas other choruses "work" only a few hours a week. These professional singers require an amazingly small number of rehearsals, even for the most difficult music. The repertory for a given season is potentially far more comprehensive than that of the ordinary chorus, especially in the field of contemporary music. These factors make the professional Chorale a useful vehicle for recording, for excessively difficult orchestral performances, and for large-scale touring on the commercial circuits across the country.

The highest paid professionals in the choral field are those singers who make the commercial jingles heard on radio and television. The next most profitable job is that in a successful Broadway musical, where dancing is required as well as singing. In the area of classical choral music, ancient and modern, the prospect that a young singer will find his niche and make a living wage remains pretty narrow, and largely a matter of chance. Some have argued for the formation of professional choral groups in key areas. "Each group would include forty singers who would be engaged for an entire season and paid by the week. Each group would devote itself wholeheartedly to a wide range of choral activities, from concerts and television appearances to working with orchestras and amateur choruses and making records."[5] But no one knows where the money for such an elaborate venture would come from.

It cannot be argued that there is a case for the small professional choir parallel to that for municipal or regional opera. The art of choral music in the United States has been well served by the amateur choruses, which in schools, colleges, and communities provide an excellent diet of choral music, rich, varied, and steadily improving in quality. Opera is, by contrast, a professional field, requiring highly skilled soloists, actors, dancers, orchestra, producers, directors, and all the trappings of the stage.

Historically, in England, Germany, and the Scandinavian countries as well as the United States, the choral field belongs to the amateurs, not to the professionals. However, in the United States, the amateurs are in for a battle with two ambitious and determined unions—AGMA, the American Guild of Musical Artists, and AFTRA, the American Federation of Television and Radio Artists. The latter has been attempting to take control of all choral recordings by symphony orchestras. The former is attempting to unionize all those singers who hope to make a professional living from choral singing, and then to force these professional choirs upon orchestras, managers, opera companies, and even churches. In an article entitled "The American Guild of Musical Artists and the Non-professional Chorus," the Executive Secretary of AGMA announced their program bluntly and boldly. The professional chorus, he said, "should be employed by the local symphony orchestras and other sponsors of musical productions such as oratorios, cantatas, etc. It should be engaged at those times in preference to amateur, college or church choirs." He adds with incomparable smugness: "This proposal could not by any stretch of the imagination be harmful to the amateur or community chorus, which could continue to perform in churches, for fraternal organizations, in factories, and at other places. The local professional, on the other hand, would be encouraged to become and remain a choral singer. His performances would also increase the understanding and appreciation of choral singing by the general musical public."[6]

One of our excellent, though smaller American orchestras, on tour through college towns, arranged for a performance of Berlioz' *L'Enfance du Christ* with the college choir in its own auditorium. Schedules for early arrival and ample rehearsal were painstakingly arranged, but AGMA refused to allow the professional orchestra to appear with the college chorus. Like the Old Testament prophet, I look upon AGMA as a cloud on the horizon no bigger than a hand, which could nonetheless overspread the whole sky to the permanent damage of our amateur choruses. There is nothing good to be said for the unionizing of choral singers. Choral singing is not a professional career nor has it any reason for existence in the commercial world. The first steps already effected in the unionization of choral singers are, I hope, tentative and experimental. Any extension should be met with the strongest opposition.

A budget for choral performance, including a salary scale for rehearsals and performances for a "symphony chorus," would constitute an impossible addition to the financial problems of symphony orchestras. Furthermore, it is doubtful whether such "professional choruses" could serve symphony orchestras as well as the amateur choruses which have collaborated with orchestras in so many cities. The unionization of choral singers would strike a mortal blow at the choral repertory of our great orchestras, and at the choral scene in general.

Variety, summing up an early (1955) attack on the New York Philharmonic by AGMA, clarified both the financial and artistic issues.

Orch may do one or two choral works a season, preferring to use a college or otherwise amateur choir, mainly because of the expense, but also *because such a chorus rehearses the work over a whole season to advantageous results.* Union wants the symph to use an AGMA chorus. For a Beethoven Ninth Symphony, which requires a chorus of about 150 in the final movement, the cost for rehearsals and a weekend of performances would run to $9,000 for singers alone. That, according to management, makes it prohibitive.[7]

Extolling the virtues of amateur choruses, Edward Tatnall Canby wrote: "the amateur fills a musical role that the professional cannot always match. . . . the best of the amateur groups can meet the best of the pros on the only ground worth discussion—perceptive, communicative performance." And: "amateur singers have long been exploring many areas of the great a cappella choral literature, which the professionals have only recently begun to enter."[8]

The movement for professional choirs, promoted by the unions and modeled on the success of the small "chorales" (a striking misuse of a noun denoting the Lutheran hymn-tune, a form of music to be sung by the whole Christian congregation), is another evidence of the American craze for virtuosi. Small professional choirs can read at sight, learn a tough piece faster, sing louder, and produce a performance in a hurry. They have their special literature, corresponding to that of the chamber orchestra; yet even this literature is equally open to the small amateur choir.

The field of choral singing, whether large choruses or small choirs, is not a hopeful outlet for young professional singers. The specialized recital literature, the solo parts in oratorio and cantata, and the long-anticipated increase of opera troupes throughout the country offer them the best opportunities.

*   *   *

The most promising career for the young instrumentalist is membership in one of the steadily multiplying number of symphony orchestras. Only the few, and not necessarily the best, will find full-time occupations as recitalists and concerto players. Even in this latter field, it is both refreshing and exciting to see one of the regular members of the orchestra step up to the spotlight and play a concerto accompanied by his colleagues. This will happen more often as the star system among instrumentalists shines less brightly. The American symphony orchestra of mid-century is, more than ever, a group of virtuosi. Contemporary orchestral literature requires a technical skill and, even more strikingly, a degree of musicianship that has narrowed the gap between concert virtuoso and orchestral player. Young professionals would be well advised to value with the utmost seriousness the training obtained in a good conservatory orchestra. Conservatory graduates in increasing numbers step directly into chairs in orchestras throughout the country. Promotions to the better-paid first desks and from orchestras in the smaller cities to the Class A metropolitan orchestras are open to the most gifted and competent. Here, rather than the recital hall, is the career for the instrumentalist.

However, orchestra salaries are still far too low. The placement office of the New England Conservatory reports that in 1959–60 the maximum salary for a graduate who found a place in one of the orchestras in his first year out was still below the minimum salary for teachers of music in the public schools. This shocking statement needs clarification. Schoolteaching requires at least thirty weeks per year, whereas orchestras in the smaller cities often play a very short season—ten, twelve, or fourteen weeks. Only the largest and most active orchestras can guarantee employment for a work-year equal to that of the teaching profession; and the Boston Symphony alone has a regular season of forty-eight weeks, offering only a month's vacation.

Orchestra players have to make part of their living by giving private lessons or by other means, hopefully musical. But there is every reason to believe that this unequal salary position will improve with the years and with recognition of the importance of good symphonic music by the general public and by municipal governments. A career combining orchestral playing and teaching in a conservatory or college is a natural solution of the financial problem if the orchestra does not maintain too rigorous a schedule. It is at this point that the academic training provided by conservatory or school of music, and certified by degrees, diplomas, or certificates, is of invaluable assistance in arranging a combined teaching-performing career. The student in conservatory or college who sacrifices his academic work for the exclusive study of his solo instrument is taking a precarious chance.

There are signs of increasing public interest in chamber music which would open up a small field of careers for string quartets as well as wind and brass ensembles, and for groups of players on old instruments, specializing in the music of the Renaissance and the Middle Ages. The great success of Noah Greenberg's group of players and singers— the New York Pro Musica Antiqua—is a demonstration of public receptiveness to ancient music presented with scholarly accuracy and a communicative sense of its timeless beauty. Old music is a new and promising field!

String quartets are most likely to succeed in the concert world if they have a specialty—the Juilliard Quartet with Bartok, the Claremont with Beethoven, and the Lenox with contemporary American and European chamber music. One hopes that an understanding of chamber music, the most aristocratic of all media, will continue to grow with the wider distribution of recordings, and that chamber music concerts will regain the popularity they had during the period of the Flonzaleys and the Kneisels. At best, however, the majority of young instrumentalists must continue to seek their fortune in the symphony orchestra.

What about pianists, the largest single division of students in the instrumental field? A few will make the concert stage, as they always have; but it is unrealistic for thousands of gifted young players to go blindly on through their conservatory course dreaming of concertos with the Boston Symphony and recitals in Carnegie Hall. Some will find careers as accompanists and chamber music players; but this too is bound to be a small number. Others will turn to the organ or the harpsichord, specialized fields of increasing significance in the musical world. Whether or not the piano be his ultimate specialty, no one need regret the time spent in perfecting his ability at the keyboard, for it is the essential work horse of the art of music and the indispensable tool of all teachers.

It must be clear from the foregoing discussion that, in my sober opinion, the talented young singer or instrumentalist should give the most earnest consideration to the career of teaching. This may seem at first a second-rate alternative to his dream of the concert stage. If he persists in this self-pity his life will be grim and his teaching ineffective. But the testimony of thousands of teachers in school, college, or conservatory refutes him. There are great rewards and human satisfactions in teaching; and his background of vocal or instrumental study, carried to a high standard, will always be a prime asset to the teacher. The concert stage is overcrowded. Teachers are in short supply. Whether in kindergarten or college, high school or conservatory, the teacher of music has the inestimable privilege of working with people and with the raw materials of beauty in his chosen art.

*   *   *

Turning from the young people with talent for performance, the executants, to those with creative gifts, the budding composers, we find another rich vein in American musical life. Hundreds of young people write music and aspire to fill the shoes of Aaron Copland and Walter Piston in their generation. There are so many young people with this gift that, if they were all to practice composition as their main business in life, the total of their output would reach an astronomical figure which would preclude the actual performance of more than a tiny fraction of what had been written! The situation is parallel to that of the oversupply of singers and instrumentalists.

The gift to scribble notes on paper or think up a new tune or splash around on the piano is almost as common as a good voice and digital dexterity. To stake all on the dream of becoming America's most famous composer in 1980 invites similar disillusion.

Walter Piston has said that no one ought to be a composer if he can possibly avoid it. This does not mean no one should write music; but it does mean that only those with the irresistible demon in them should dedicate themselves to the life of the professional composer. Only those willing to pay the price will submit to the long and arduous discipline of learning the craft of composition. The cost, not only in money, but still more in the most intense self-discipline, is great. The way is hard, and the outcome is uncertain.

What, then, should the young man or woman do, who loves to write and who cannot help it? He has three choices: to seek out a private composition teacher for whom he might be both pupil and apprentice; to enroll in a conservatory; or to go to college. Between the last two, the deciding factor should be the student's preference for the general climate and atmosphere, more professional in the conservatory, more liberal in the university. What of his career after conservatory or college? Few have made a living in the twentieth century as composers alone. Why should we be surprised, and why should we deplore this fact? Bach, Mozart, Palestrina, Byrd, Machaut, Purcell, Monteverdi, and Gabrieli were "composers on the side." Call the roll of the creative figures of history; they were choirmasters or conductors or performers or teachers. Bach taught Latin as well as music in the choir school of St. Thomas Church. He conducted the orchestra and trained the singers; indeed he was so busy, day in and day out, that it is hard to see how he composed anything. Yet he had the craftsmanship, the know-how, and the gift to write an amazing amount of beautiful music. Mahler conducted opera all over Europe and at the Metropolitan, and in his last years he was Music Director of the New York Philharmonic; yet he found time for nine symphonies and sketches for a tenth. Paul Hindemith, Gustav Holst, Ralph Vaughan Williams, Walter Piston, William Schuman—all have been teachers. Walter Piston has written about the composer as teacher:

In my opinion experience has shown that a teacher's job is a good job for most composers. Experience has also shown that it is a poor job for those who take it solely as a means of livelihood. Unless he is interested in teaching, a composer will be both an unhappy and an unsuccessful teacher, not to mention the insincerity of his position. He had better spend designated hours making perfunctory motions in some mechanical employment . . .

Teaching is time-consuming. This is really serious, there is no doubt about it. . . . When we realize how much our thoughts are preoccupied with matters related to the job, we see that teaching can easily become, and often does, a one hundred per cent full-time occupation. All that can be said on the other side is that any job takes time, and that the problem can be solved through the resourcefulness and strength of will of the individual. This has been proven by numerous examples among composers. . . .

The daily association with young, alert and creative minds cannot be overrated as a beneficial force against growing stale. . . . Indeed, it has happened more than once that teacher and student have lost their identities and the roles have gotten interchanged. Teaching and learning are far from being opposites.[9]

The ivory-tower composer who has no other musical job in life is largely an invention of the romantic nineteenth century; he is not typical in the history of music. Yet those who are most eager to help our young composers, to foster creative talent, dream of larger and larger commissions, more and more "free time to compose." What the composer needs is not so much subsidies, fellowships, but the opportunity to have his music played and a sympathetic hearing for it. If the energy and argument and money that go into subsidizing the composer could be devoted to more performances of his work, and to the education of the public so that they would understand and respond to his work, he would be a happier man.

"Composers-in-residence" on college campuses should teach—on a light schedule one would hope—but let them teach theory; let them expound the twentieth-century technique of composition for the college amateurs as well as young students of composition; and let them conduct some of their own music with college orchestras and choruses.

The anomaly called "composer-in-residence" is an institution of such recent origin that it may well be an injustice to say that it seems to me an ignominious position for a composer. The business of an educational institution is education and if the kept composer does only composing, what does the institution get out of it? If the composer teaches, in any sense, and I should think he would want to earn his keep, the situation ought to be dignified by a suitable academic appointment.[10]

The best that the United States can do for its composers is to give them jobs for which their qualifications fit them— and then bend every effort to get a hearing for their compositions, and not only a single first performance but a second and a third and, one would hope, a fifteenth and a twenty-fifth. This takes money, and here the foundations and the wealthy patrons can and must help. It also requires a musical public with curiosity, tolerance, persistence, and above all eagerness—eagerness to hear new works and to hear them again and again. It calls for a major shift in the make-up of programs in symphony concerts, chamber music, piano recitals, and even opera. It is in this general area of education and promotion that the music critic, the journalist, the editor, the teacher, and the champion of good causes can do more than anyone else for the composer of the middle twentieth century. There is no short cut, no royal road for the American composer. Those who are eager to help should work, not on subsidies, but on the everlasting job of getting scores performed, recorded, and widely distributed. Here, as in school music and in church music, the answer is the education of the public.

* * *

I have pointed out that the number of gifted children is enormous. Beautiful voices are, in the vernacular, a dime

a dozen. Talented pianists, violinists, and cellists, are nearly
as plentiful. Hundreds can write music and want to be
composers. There is not room at the top for more than a
fraction of those whose natural gifts, if well nurtured and
properly trained, would justify a place at that lofty pinnacle.
There is an overpopulation of talent good enough for the
summit—if the summit is defined as the Metropolitan
Opera for singers, the stage of Carnegie Hall for pianists,
and the mantle of Aaron Copland for composers. Furthermore, the stern fact remains that, contrary to what warm-
hearted friends of music have said, the world does not owe
these gifted musicians anything but a good job.

Tragedies of disappointment, frustration, and despair
are found everywhere along the road, from the young prodigy to the virtuoso who just barely missed the grand prize
in one of the great competitions. What is most tragic is that
these young people want to be in music because they love
it. They are attracted by fame and fortune, but way down
deep it is the love of music that makes them want to spend
their lives at it.

They can. This is the good news of the twentieth century. Where the pinnacle is brutally crowded, the lower
ranks are crying out for recruits. I say to the young lover
of music who wants to spend his life at it: enlist in the
ranks. There are many careers in music, new and old. The
oldest and the most honorable and possibly the very happi-
est of all is that of the teacher. But there are new careers in
music undreamed of a generation ago.[11] The number of
American orchestras has increased enormously; each requires not only players but a staff—librarians, managers,
secretaries, a radio expert, a program-book editor. These
people spend their lives inside a great musical organism and
are, in the truest sense, colleagues of the conductors and
the players.

Consider the vast field of radio, television, and recording. The music director at a recording session, who sits at the dials with the score before him, is a more powerful figure at that moment than the conductor on the stage. He needs not only scientific craftsmanship, but impeccable taste in music, and a vast knowledge of history, style, structure, texture, and orchestration. The producer of symphony broadcasts and television shows must be a man with scientific know-how and also the most sensitive musicianship. The program director of a good music station serves as the mediator, the guiding intelligence between the vast store of music literature and the public.

One of the older careers, and yet hardly a half-century old in the United States, is that of music librarian. I can remember when the Music Library Association was founded with no more than a handful of members. Now there are hundreds of special music librarians in the country. Music rooms and record collections have been added to public libraries. College and conservatory music libraries are continually increasing their staffs. The New York Public Library and the Library of Congress contain music divisions with a variety of experts on subjects as varied as medieval paleography, folk-song archives, and contemporary recordings on tape—the material for a future history of music in the twentieth century. Research in electronics and acoustics or manuscripts and codices offers examples of other professional activities in music. Scientific and learned careers growing out of nineteenth-century acoustics and musicology have expanded enormously in the twentieth century.

The music publishing business requires scholarship of a high order and expert knowledge in a variety of fields, as do journalism and criticism. Museum work in music embraces two areas: the care and preservation of ancient instruments and musical manuscripts, demanding expert curators; and music education departments, which are on the increase, following the pioneer work of the Toledo Museum of Art. Curators, librarians, and journalists are not primarily performers; yet men and women follow such careers because they love music and want to devote their lives to it.

Finally, I have known many lovers of music—gifted pianists, excellent violinists, and good cellists—who decided to make music not their profession but their avocation. String quartets have become a speciality among doctors and surgeons. Groups of madrigal singers and groups of recorder players, not to mention choral singers the country over and players in civic orchestras—these are not professionals who have not made the grade but musicians who have found a happy life in which music and the making of music is an avocation, a recreation in the truest and deepest sense.

Music is a vaster field than in the time of our fathers. Far more jobs are available than ever before. But the number of positions for virtuosi remains constant or has declined. The strategy for our time is to downgrade the emphasis on the summit and to upgrade the importance of music practitioners in a wide variety of careers. This is a new phenomenon, not widely understood. The responsibility rests squarely on the parents of gifted children, on teachers and counselors in elementary and secondary schools, on school principals and college advisors, and above all on the music teachers, into whose hands come the precious gifts of young lives with talent and promise and a deep love of music. The talent may be outstanding or it may be small. The evaluation should not be made lightly, for on that evaluation and on the guidance of the talented child depends a life of frustration and disappointment or a life of usefulness, of satisfaction, and of joy in the world of music.

𝕮𝕳𝕬𝕻𝕿𝕰𝕽 𝖁𝕴𝕴 · SCHOLAR AND TEACHER

FROM THE EARLIEST times music has been a field of learning and scholarship; yet in the United States this is one of its most recent and most misunderstood manifestations. The musician is recognized as composer or performer or critic or teacher, but what of the musician as scholar? The image—to use that overworked word only once on these pages—of the musicologist in the American mind is often unclear or disparaging. "He doesn't make music; he only writes books about it." Even college presidents are apt to think of music as composition and performance exclusively. The failure of deans and faculties to recognize musicology is a paradox, for if music be in any sense a learned discipline, it is precisely that area of the subject that belongs within the university. The spectacle of a community of scholars looking on music solely as a creative and performing art is vivid evidence of the late arrival of musical scholarship in the United States. The continued misunderstanding of the boundaries of musicology is all too evident from the application of the term to a variety of academic courses not properly described as musicological, and from the indiscriminate granting of the Ph.D. degree in many American universities for any and all forms of advanced training in music.

For the Greeks, music was a field of systematic study and analysis, related to philosophy and mathematics. In the Middle Ages, it was one of the four subjects in the *quadrivium*—astronomy, arithmetic, geometry, and music—

and, as such, a regular part of the curriculum for the early Masters of Arts. Some of the most important treatises on music theory come from the Middle Ages. The mention of a few titles reveals their depth and variety; they are learned, philosophical, scientific, and practical—but *not* primarily historical.

Sixth century: Boethius, *De institutione musica*
Eleventh century: Guido d'Arezzo, *Micrologus*
About 1300: Walter Odington, *De speculatione musicae*
About 1320: Philippe de Vitry, *Ars nova*
1477: Johannes Tinctoris, *Liber de arte contrapuncti*
1496: Franchino Gafori, *Practica musicae*
1511: Arnold Schlick, *Spiegel der Orgelmacher und Organister*
1511: Sebastian Virdung, *Musica getutscht*
1532: Martin Agricola, *Musica figuralis deudsch*
1547: Heinrich Glareanus, *Dodecachordon*
1558: Gioseffo Zarlino, *Le istitutioni harmoniche*
1581: Vincenzo Galilei, *Dialogo . . . della musica antica e della moderna*

Similar tracts appeared in increasing numbers throughout the Renaissance, the Baroque, and the classical periods. Dr. Burney's *General History of Music* (four volumes, 1776 to 1789) was one of the earliest books to be concerned not so much with the science and philosophy of music, but specifically with its history.[1] Since that time musicology has been predominantly a historical discipline.

Musicology is a relatively new word in the English language, an adaptation from the French term *musicologie*. The German *Musikwissenschaft* was used for the first time only about a hundred years ago by Chrysander, one of the earlier professional music historians. The term musicology denotes both scientific and historical study, the systematic organization of knowledge about music. As a scholarly discipline music has frontiers of knowledge waiting to be pushed further and further back through new discoveries.

Research involves not only the discovery of new facts but also the exhaustive apparatus of analysis, categories, systems, and the orderly arrangement of facts, plus the exegesis of the meaning of facts. There is an invisible line between historical musicology and art criticism, although it is possible to distinguish between them at the opposite ends of the spectrum.

The modern history of musicology begins in the German universities in the nineteenth century. It sprang from a curiosity about the past, especially the Middle Ages and the Renaissance. One of its earliest monuments is Winterfeld's investigation of Giovanni Gabrieli and the glories of Venetian musical art, a work which came out in 1834.[2] By 1860 the movement was in full swing, its followers fired with the determination to recover and to publish music which had long been lost. The middle of the century marks the launching of extensive projects in publication: the musical paleography of the Middle Ages, collections of early chant, and especially the complete works of Bach, Handel, Palestrina, Lassus, and many other composers of the sixteenth, seventeenth, and eighteenth centuries. Some of these complete editions are, even today, far from complete—Purcell, for example—and the ceaseless quest for documents, autographs, manuscripts, and first editions continues. Scholarly publications were often national in their orientation— Monuments of German Music (*Denkmäler deutscher Tonkunst*), Monuments of Bavarian Music (*Denkmäler der Tonkunst in Bayern*), Monuments of Musical Art in Austria (*Denkmäler der Tonkunst in Oesterreich*), *The English Madrigal School, Les Maîtres Musiciens de la Renaissance Française, Istituzioni e Monumenti dell'Arte Musicale Italiana*, and many more.[3]

The recovery of manuscript and printed sources, and the scholarly publication of music from the past is but one area of musicology. As soon as the music became available, scholars began work on historical, critical, and analytical studies, together with monographs on *Aufführungspraxis*, dealing with the actual conditions and methods of performance. These historical, critical, and analytical works form the central core of the learned literature about music. Max Loehr, in his Inaugural Lecture as Rockefeller Professor of Oriental Art at Harvard, said: "The business of the art historian is to understand the objects he studies."[4] This is a simple definition, yet its realization is paradoxically complex. To understand the objects, whether they be Chinese paintings or Renaissance motets, requires an understanding of the background, the culture of the time, the relation of the particular objects to the common practices of the time, the conditions of performance, and an all-encompassing analysis of style. As a vast and varied literature, music invites the historical approach, the most exacting scholarly discipline, and the entire apparatus and insight of style criticism.

The study of the literature of music requires the discovery and accurate reproduction of the monuments themselves. Historical musicology therefore includes at the very outset the related fields of paleography, musical notation, and the history, construction, and sonority of instruments. Each is a substantial territory of research. Take for example the question of instrumental music in the Middle Ages. Older histories of music claimed that there was practically no instrumental music before the sixteenth century, and that what there was had no aesthetic value. As recently as 1904 a reputable history made the following categorical statement: "In Palestrina's time instrumental music had scarcely begun, and there were hardly any instruments sufficiently well constructed to play anything worthy of the name of music upon."[5] This is a classic example of a

historical generalization refuted a hundred times by research during the last fifty years. We now know that there
were instruments and instrumental music centuries before
the Renaissance, and that the music was of great beauty.
We owe this knowledge to three different kinds of musicians
—the research scholars, the craftsmen who have rebuilt the
old instruments, and the performers who have mastered the
technique of the instruments and given us a chance to hear
the old music. Evidences of instrumental music before 1500
have been drawn from the decorative arts—painting, sculpture, and miniatures and decorations in manuscripts—as
well as from countless literary references and actual examples of music.

In the area of historical research, contemporary books
about the music of a given period are just as important as
the music itself. There is a long line of theoretical treatises
and instruction books, telling how to compose music and
how to play each of the instruments—for example, how to
realize the figured bass and how to play the ornaments in
the time of Bach. These contemporary theory books are
indispensable to the understanding of early music and its
performance.

Historical musicology and the solutions of its problems
involve paleography, the study of music in relation to the
visual arts, the history of theory, the study of notation and
of instruments, the study of contemporary aesthetics, and
always the everlasting search for materials. Here is a vast
orbit of musical activities, and for a hundred years scores of
musicians have spent their lives in these studies. Yet musicology remains for the most part unknown to the general
public and unrecognized as a vital part of the musical profession.

*　　*　　*

Outside the strictly historical field, there are a number of related scientific disciplines. Acoustics is the science of sound, with a history stretching from Pythagoras through the tempered scale to Philharmonic Hall.* It is not only a pure or theoretical science, but an applied science, embracing the entire area of musical instruments, from organ pipes to the tuning of a violin string and the production of horn notes. Electronics is as new as acoustics is old, and it is the source of the entire field of recordings, radio, television, and electronic music. Physiology and psychology each embrace a body of scientific literature related to music, whereas aesthetics, with a continuous history from the Greeks to contemporary philosophy, remains closer to criticism than musicology.

I include architecture as a related discipline because architects and musicians have been notoriously ignorant of each other, notwithstanding the fact that the actual sound of music depends, not only on the instrument which makes it, but equally on the room in which it is made. The wondrous sound of Renaissance motets performed by a choir in the east end of a Gothic or Romanesque cathedral (or in a small village church built of stone), a sonority richly blended yet clear in all its parts, is an example of the perfect adjustment between the compositional technique of the music and its architectural surroundings. Similar examples of perfection would be the symphonic repertory of the last two centuries performed by the Boston Symphony Orchestra in Symphony Hall, or the Philadelphia Orchestra in the Academy of Music. Architects, acoustical engineers, and musicians can join forces to produce the most beautiful results; or they can ignore each other or refuse to cooperate,

* Despite the most up-to-date scientific planning, the acoustics of Philharmonic Hall in the Lincoln Center for the Performing Arts, New York (opened in September 1962) revealed numerous defects during its first season.

with calamitous consequences. Contemporary scientists, for example, have designed buildings where the acoustics are so brutally clear that you can hear the crinkling noise of the paper when the violinists in the orchestra turn their pages. The familiar sound when a letter is opened and read in the movies becomes a meddlesome intrusion in a Mozart symphony. In both instances the studio is too dry.

One of the newer fields within the area of musicology per se is the study of the music of other cultures—the Far East, Indonesia, India, and Africa. Only a few years ago this study was referred to as comparative musicology or "primitive" music. The commonly accepted term now is ethnomusicology, which links this aspect of musical research with the disciplines of ethnology and anthropology. The study embraces all those aspects of research which had previously been applied to the history and performance of European music. The number of young students interested in the field is steadily increasing; there are more systematic courses on ethnomusicology in our colleges; and there will be more of this music heard in the Western world. One performance of *gamelan* music or the music of Japan, China, or India is enough to convince the sensitive listener that the term primitive music is a misnomer. Each of these ethnographic traditions represents a highly complex and mature art form. Since it is not western, our predecessors called it primitive, at the same time maintaining illogically that music is a universal language. We are decades behind our colleagues in the visual arts in recognizing the validity of music outside our tradition, music with its own language, rhetoric, and literature. When we do recognize it for what it is, we shall have the ethnomusicologists to thank.

*   *   *

Music as a learned discipline belongs primarily in the college and university, in association with other learned disciplines and in a climate where research is fostered and the methods of research are common practice. It was less than a hundred years ago that President Eliot of Harvard appointed John Knowles Paine to the first chair of music in an American university. Paine was no musicologist, although it is recorded that for his organ recitals in the old Boston Music Hall, he never played anything but J. S. Bach, then regarded as "ancient" music.

The Musical Quarterly, the finest scholarly periodical on music published in America, was launched in January 1915. Waldo Selden Pratt wrote the first article in the first issue, with the title "On Behalf of Musicology." His last paragraph was prophetic.

It is likely that no one person, in these days of advanced specialism, can hope to be a full master of details in all branches of what has been called "musicology" . . . or to be engaged in fruitful original discovery in many lines. But it is not too much to hope that more disciplined scholars in the musical circle will so familiarize themselves with the total range of the subject that they can, in their own persons and work, commend the science of music to the attention of both the scientific and the artistic worlds. It may even be that sometime there will be in the faculties of certain large institutions a professorship of "musicology," whose function shall be to unfold the broad outlines of the science and to demonstrate not only its intellectual dignity among other sciences, but its practical utility on a large scale to hosts of musicians and music lovers.[6]

In 1929 the American Council of Learned Societies appointed a committee on musicology, and in 1932 this committee published a bulletin by Oliver Strunk, "The State and Resources of Musicology in the United States."[7] Two years later, 1934, the American Musicological Society was founded, with Otto Kinkeldey as its first president. Among a notable company of American scholars—Pratt, Carl Engel, Charles Seeger, and others—Kinkeldey has always been regarded as the dean.

In 1939, just at the time of the outbreak of the war in Europe, an international congress of musicology was held in New York, and again in September 1961, the International Musicological Society returned to the United States for meetings in New York, New Haven, Princeton, and Washington. In the period of the thirties and the forties, a series of European scholars of music made their way to the United States as refugees and greatly enriched our musical life. Possibly the most eminent and beneficent of these were Alfred Einstein who settled at Smith College in the Connecticut Valley, Curt Sachs at New York University, and Manfred Bukofzer at the University of California in Berkeley. The invention of microfilm has made it possible to bring immense quantities of basic material from Europe to libraries in the United States, and it is fortunate that some of this transfer took place before the Second World War, thus preserving monuments which might otherwise have been lost.

From the day of its entrance into American colleges and universities, the very diversity of musical art has been the occasion of stresses and strains in the academic world. The existence of two separate societies of college music teachers during the late forties and fifties is evidence of the rivalry of academic and applied music, of the scholar and the performer. Henry Purcell, in the preface to his *Twelve Sonnatas of Three Parts,* published in London in 1683, warned the reader at the outset that he would refrain from "an elaborate harangue on the beauty and the charms of Musick," because, he added, "(after all the learned Encomions that words can contrive) [music] commends itself best by the performances of a skilful hand, and an angelical voice."[8] The antithesis, so quaintly suggested by Purcell, between learned commentary and actual performance, is an idea which crops up constantly in writings upon music. It is found in the remarkable preface to American musicology by Dr. Pratt, from which I have already quoted. It appeared to him that there was nothing less than "a chasm between the artistic and the scientific worker." He pointed out, however, that the most intimate relations between the theoretical and the applied exist in other fields, for example between the science of chemistry and the art of medicine. And he observed that, "when once an artist in any field has exercised his mind scientifically, or a scientist has sought for artistic accomplishment, he is bound to see that the two sorts of mental operation are not only equally normal and delightful, but that both are essential to well-rounded mentality. They are complementary, not antagonistic."[9]

It is no good denying the tendency toward abstraction which still exists among researchers, and the blind distrust of both the historical and the analytical approach to music on the part of some performers and listeners. On the one hand, there is the vast area of historical, analytical, and theoretical investigation; on the other, the enormous, practical business of music making. The scientific mind and the artistic mind each pursues its own orbit, with a great gulf between them.

Yet scholarship has contributions to make to the performer. The moral obligation of the performer of music is unique; he is the mediator through whom, and through whom alone, the work of the composer is made manifest. The painter or the sculptor records his ideas in such form that they may be directly perceived by the beholder. The ideas of the composer must be conveyed to the listener through the double phenomena of notation and recurring and variable performances. To perform a piece of music "in the style" is to reproduce as faithfully as possible the essential elements of the composer's conception in their own terms. To borrow a phrase from phonograph engineering, a high-fidelity performance is the inescapable obligation of the artist. The progressive revelation of the "own terms" of the composer's conception constitutes the most direct contribution of the musicologist to the practical musician. It is only misunderstanding and prejudice that fixes the gulf between scholar and performer. There should be the closest and most intimate cooperation, and happily progress has been made in this good cause since Dr. Pratt sounded the first call in 1915.

* * *

Music is a latecomer in the academic family. There is still no agreement on its proper orbit in the university. Nowhere is this clearer than in the indiscriminate use or misuse of the Ph.D. degree as the uniform certificate of the completion of graduate study in music. The uniformity and universality of this requirement is not in accord with the realities of the situation. Music is a field of learning, a scholarly discipline, and as such, the doctorate in philosophy in music is just as appropriate as a Ph.D. in English literature, economic history, or chemistry. Music is also an art, the creative art of composition, the re-creative art of performance. It is a craft, and craftsmanship is something quite different from research and the systematic organization of knowledge.

Far too many colleges require a doctorate for appointments and for promotions to a higher rank in the music faculty. It has been my observation as placement officer of the Department of Music at Harvard that the larger universities, in announcing vacancies on their staff, often ignore the degree, whereas the smaller and less well-known colleges, needing a status symbol, insist upon it. Three notices recently received—one for a teacher of class piano, another for music appreciation for the general college student, and a third for private cello, ear training, sight singing, and keyboard harmony—all added the ridiculous phrase "doctorate essential."

The Ph.D. should not be the sole standard of measurement in so varied an art as music. In many academic fields the doctor's degree is the common symbol of the completion of graduate training, whereas in music many of the best men go abroad for a period of European study directly after the completion of their master's degree program, and sometimes immediately after receiving the bachelor's degree. Many of them study in Paris, others hold fellowships in the American Academy in Rome, and others study their special field—composition, performance, or conducting—elsewhere. A few of these men return to an American university and take a doctor's degree, with a dissertation in some field of research in musicology. For the great majority, however, formal education is completed at the end of the period of European study. Measured by age (which is a factor not to be neglected), maturity, and mastery of their field, these young men have equaled, with their more diverse training, the normal stage of advancement recognized by the award of a doctor's degree in the field of musicology.

The requirement of the Ph.D. as the union card for college teaching has caused concern in other fields where, as in music, the degree ought to be reserved for research and pure scholarship. In January 1961 the American Mathematical Society and the Mathematical Association of America recommended a completely new degree in mathematics, the Doctor of Arts in Mathematics, based on a program of graduate studies which, though different in emphasis, would equal the Ph.D. in quality and rigor. It would be less geared to research and aimed more directly toward general equipment for college teaching.

A few American universities have instituted a somewhat similar music degree, the Doctor of Musical Arts. Stanford University announced:

The purpose of the Doctor of Musical Arts program is to offer advanced training in the practice of music parallel to the musicological studies leading to the Ph.D. degree. Students may concentrate in composition, conducting, performance practice in early music, or music education. Each concentration, however, will be given breadth through collateral studies in other branches of music and in relevant fields outside music. In all cases the work is planned especially with regard to possible careers in college or university teaching.[10]

I am not suggesting for a moment that the composer or performer or conductor, the craftsman in music, should sidestep or bypass all scholarly training. What I am advocating is that there be a variety of graduate programs in music, each with high standards of excellence, and its appropriate academic mark of distinction.

(1) The Ph.D. should be reserved for programs of study culminating in a scholarly dissertation which lies clearly in the field of musicology as I have defined it.

(2) The new Doctor of Musical Arts degree, not the Ph.D., is appropriate for composition, conducting, and advanced work in theory. It should be noted that a Doctorate of Musical Arts does not certify an original creator-composer, but does indicate that the candidate has mastered the advanced stages of the craft of musical composition.

(3) Research in music education should lead to the degree Doctor of Education rather than either Ph.D. or Doctor of Musical Arts.

(4) Performance should be recognized in the traditional

way at the lower levels by the degrees Bachelor of Music and Master of Music, and at the highest level by some such award as Artist's Diploma, which already exists in some schools and conservatories, and signifies the attainment of great distinction.

Finally—and this is the all-important corollary—the Ph.D. should not be the sole qualification for a teaching job. The degree should be restored to its proper connotation and full dignity; and other accomplishments and qualifications in music should be given their own significant and historic recognition.

The successful completion of formal education at the graduate level means not just one thing, but any one of several things, such as the conclusion of a period of European study, or notable attainment in the craft of composition or performance or conducting. A job candidate should be evaluated in terms of his total equipment, professional and human, for the post to be filled—be it college organist, teacher of advanced composition, choral conductor, or director of graduate studies in research. Since the orbit of music in a college or university covers music as a performing art, a creative art, a literature, and one of the humanities, as well as a field of learning, let each job be awarded to the man best qualified. The uniform demand for the Ph.D. has already debased the coin, and many of these degrees are third-rate or quite meaningless. In the words of Don Alhambra's song in *The Gondoliers:*

> In short, whoever you may be
> To this conclusion you'll agree,
> When every one is somebodee,
> Then no one's anybody![11]

*　　*　　*

I rate the teaching of music a career second to none in importance for the community and in happiness for the musician. I make no distinction between the teacher in schools, elementary and secondary, the teacher in conservatories, colleges, and universities, and the so-called private teacher. I include also the choirmasters in churches and choral and orchestral conductors, whose main business is education, and I include music critics and journalists insofar as they fulfill their functions as teachers. Composers and performers we shall always have. Scholars and musicologists are coming to the surface in increasing numbers in our graduate schools. Many other careers in music are opening up in the middle twentieth century. But good teachers are scarce. As a nation we are entering a period when the upsurge of public interest in music makes the recruitment of teachers a desperate need. To find and train able teachers in an era of unprecedented expansion is a paramount task for all those concerned with the future of music in America. If teachers with the best training and the highest standards are not found, the vacuum will be filled by inferior teachers with low standards, and the progress of a half-century will be rolled back in a flood of mediocrity.

Having in mind not only the training of professionals in the old and the new careers in music, but also the needs of that army which Jacques Barzun calls "the indispensable amateurs," what are the essentials and what are the nonessentials in the preparation for a job in teaching music? The first requisite is the ability to play the piano so that it is available as a tool in all kinds of study and teaching. Secondly, a general knowledge of the history and theory of music should be the common equipment of all teachers, plus a precise knowledge of certain areas and certain crafts, differing for each person and ranging all the way from the teaching of children in the kindergarten to graduate instruction in canon and fugue or research in medieval music. A third practical qualification for the great majority of school and college jobs is a knowledge of the craft of conducting plus a background of experience in choral singing or orchestral playing. And the fourth is a discriminating taste, high standards in the choice of music, the gift of radiating a love of the best, and that mysterious quality of creative imagination which makes teaching not only a job but a fine art.

The nonessentials are doctorates, except for those whose work is going to be research and the guidance of research; and a heavy indoctrination of education courses, except where they are specifically required for teaching certificates.

It is clear enough how the first three essentials may be acquired. But what about the fourth, the mysterious quality of creative imagination? Some say that people are either born with it or not, that it cannot be acquired. I disagree. In talking with my students about this intimate but vital part of their preparation I have often referred them to two great books, Whitehead's *Aims of Education* and Lowes's *The Road to Xanadu*. Whitehead has a chapter on the "Rhythm of Education" in which he speaks of the three stages of mental growth: the stage of romance, the stage of precision, and the stage of generalization. The stage of precision embraces the facts and formulas, the methods and techniques, the crafts and skills in the equipment of the teacher. These he must have. But Whitehead says, "It is evident that a stage of precision is barren without a previous stage of romance." And he says of the stage of generalization, "It is a return to romanticism with the added advantage of classified ideas and relevant technique. It is the fruition which has been the goal of the precise training." Then he makes the most important point of all: "Education should consist in a continual repetition of such cycles. Each lesson in its minor way should form an eddy cycle issuing in its own subordinate process."[12]

The academic curriculum is geared mainly to the stage of precision. This is right and proper; but it is not enough. The other two stages, the stage of romance and the stage of generalization, depend absolutely upon that creative imagination which I set down as the fourth essential for the teacher. The best study of the creative imagination that I know is John Livingston Lowes's *The Road to Xanadu*. Lowes started out with all the scholarly paraphernalia of literary research to uncover the "sources" of "The Rime of the Ancient Mariner" and "Kubla Khan." But his book brings us "ultimately to the workings of the imaginative energy itself."[13] The titles of the first few chapters are suggestive: "Chaos," "The Falcon's Eye," "The Deep Well," "The Shaping Spirit," "The Magical Synthesis." The heart of the matter comes in the chapter on the Deep Well. There is, he says,

a process which, it would seem, goes on with peculiar intensity in a poet's mind and which in Coleridge's case apparently went on incessantly. One after another vivid bits from what *he* read dropped into that deep well. And there, below the level of conscious mental processes, they set up their obscure and powerful reactions. . . . The creatures of the great deep had become the new creation of a yet deeper deep. And when the flash of inspiration at last came . . .

> They moved in tracks of shining white,
> And when they reared, the elfish light
> Fell off in hoary flakes . . .
> Blue, glossy green, and velvet black,
> They coil'd and swam; and every track
> Was a flash of golden fire.

No mortal eye had ever seen them actually coil and swim . . . in the waters of any earthly sea. They were the birth of that

creative deep, which is peculiar to the poet only in degree. . . .
The imagination "dissolves, diffuses, dissipates, in order to
re-create." . . .
Out of the heart of the chaos sprang the poems.[14]

So much for Coleridge and "The Rime of the Ancient
Mariner." But Lowes said that "The Deep Well" is "peculiar
to the poet only in degree. . . . [It] underlies your consciousness and mine."[15] And his whole thesis applies to music as
well as to poetry, and above all to the art of teaching.
Whitehead's stage of romance and stage of generalization
come from the Deep Well and from nowhere else. Out of
that chaos come the flashes of inspiration and insight, those
mysteries of the creative imagination which characterize
the gifted teacher.

The old Quaker college in Richmond, Indiana—Earlham
College—has a sentence carved in stone over the great fireplace in the dining room. It comes from the logbook of one
of the little ships which set sail from England to carry a
group of emigrants from the Society of Friends to the shores
of the New World. They sailed along the coast of their
homeland for a day, and put back for one last stop before
heading out across the western ocean. The logbook, and
now the Earlham fireplace, records this sentence: "We
gathered sticks, and kindled a fire, and left it burning."
To kindle a fire, and leave it burning—that is the aim of all
great teachers, but most of all, perhaps, the teacher of
music.

CHAPTER VIII · THE MUSIC CRITIC

THE MUSIC CRITIC is a man who thinks and writes about music. Well, aren't we all? At least we all talk about music, even if we don't write about it, or think too deeply about it. Virgil Thomson, at once composer and critic, said at the Harvard Symposium on Criticism in 1947: "The instinct for judging music is universal."[1] What I have to say, therefore, about the professional journalist applies in varying degree through the whole spectrum, from the casual comment of the amateur to the erudite exposition of the scholar.

Criticism is simply the ability to say something about the meaning and the value of an object. Criticism is commentary; it represents a human reaction to an event, a painting, or a piece of music. The more we know about the object of our criticism, the better we can put into words our comment and our judgment. I say "put into words"; criticism is a verbal art, whether written or spoken. We ought to be able to "state the case" for a piece of music; or if we are not able to do so we should like to be able to do so. Criticism is neither constructive nor destructive, as is so often claimed by those who raise a hue and cry about it. It involves no more than stating the case, putting a performance or a piece of music in its place among all other possible performances and all other pieces.

Too often the amateur waits for the morning paper to state the case for him. Igor Stravinsky, that most professional of professionals, said with respect to the position of the public vis-à-vis the professional critic: "the public always has, if not talent, . . . at least, when it is left to itself, a spontaneity that confers great value upon its reactions." And he added, "provided again that it has not been contaminated with the virus of snobbery."[2]

In the first chapter of this book I called attention to the enormous growth in the number of concertgoers, record collectors, radio listeners, and television viewers. It follows that the potential number of readers and talkers about music has vastly multiplied; and there is no doubt that talk about music among nonprofessionals has increased greatly. How intelligent this talk or criticism may be and how widespread is the knowledge and background necessary to give a sound basis for balanced judgment are questions about which, even in this statistical age, we have no reliable information. Alfred Einstein, writing about Mozart's extraordinary handling of symphonic form, said:

Everything seems familiar and popular; yet at every instant there are surprises, an exuberance of spirit and a feeling of power, and unexpected refinements. . . . The nineteenth century gradually lost any understanding for such things, since it had lost the feeling for any definite framework, or any given forms. But Mozart's public included some listeners who could appreciate every subtle divergence from the expected.[3]

It is my belief that, if the nineteenth century lost such connoisseurs, they have come back in the twentieth century. Scattered through the vast population of listeners are an increasing number of gifted and sensitive persons who can understand and appreciate "every subtle divergence from the expected." They are the people who play their records over and over again until they know each measure as well as the performer, who never miss a symphony concert, who have read Copland's *What to Listen for in Music*,[4] or something not quite so good as that most excellent book! These people talk about music, and their talk is often highly intelligent and in the best sense critical.

It is a disheartening paradox that, despite the new army of concertgoers and listeners, the amount of space devoted to music in the daily newspapers has suffered a steady curtailment in the last forty years. There are new hi-fi magazines and record reviews. Periodicals such as *The New Yorker, The Saturday Review,* and *The Atlantic* give far more attention to music than formerly, both in the conventional field of concert reviews and the new field of record criticism. But newspaper space has been steadily shrinking. The theater, the movies, concerts and recitals are lumped together; available space for all three is assigned on the basis of attendance—movies versus theater versus music. If attendance figures alone are to determine the distribution of newspaper space we have little to hope for from the daily press. Reviews of new movies run to ten or twelve times as many inches as are allotted to concerts and records combined. Television reviews have consumed more and more of the precious space available, concerts are neglected, and the amount assigned to radio performances of good music is just about zero.

Music needs more space in the newspapers. Those who control such matters would answer that this depends entirely upon the public. Although I think the editors and publishers have in recent years made a niggardly estimate of the public demand for music news, considering the vast increase in the number of people interested in music, the fact remains that all those desirous of music news and criticism in the daily press must take a stand and express their views.

* * *

What are the qualities we look for in a great music critic?

A love of music and the capacity for the most intense feeling about art.

A wide knowledge of the history, literature, and theory of music.

A minimum of prejudice and a maximum of curiosity, tolerance, humility, and imagination.

A passion for communication, for teaching.

A love of writing for its own sake, and some gift for it.

Obviously skill in verbalism is of primary importance for the critic. He must employ words efficiently to meet space requirements. Vividness and imagination are equally important, and they belong to the critic only in degree. The teacher of children, the choral conductor, the contemporary composer, the intelligent guest at a dinner-table conversation—all of us, professionals and amateurs alike, need the gift of verbal description. You cannot put the music into words, yet you must. Happy are those who have a flair for it!

I remember Koussevitzky rehearsing the *Istar Variations* of D'Indy with the Boston Symphony Orchestra. The variations end with a glowing passage, neither loud nor soft, neither fast nor slow, a balanced, steady *mezzo forte* with no rise or fall, moving serenely through the epilogue to a luminous F-major ending. The whole orchestra is playing, without addition or subtraction of instruments, a *tutti* of brass, woodwinds, strings, and percussion. Koussevitzky kept stopping the orchestra to ask for more clarinet, less bassoon, more vibrato in the strings, just the right amount of timpani, a little quieter trumpets and trombones. Finally he put down his stick and said, "Gentlemen, you give me a sonority of clarinets, and a sonority of bassoons, a sonority of violas, a sonority of trumpets." And then, with a great encircling gesture, "It must be *a sonority of gold.*" The most precise technical directions, addressed to a most expert body of professional musicians, had not done the trick; but

I shall never forget the extraordinary sound which was somehow achieved by Koussevitzky's flash of imaginative description.

Donald Francis Tovey, writing of that extraordinary passage at the end of the development and the beginning of the recapitulation in the first movement of Brahms' *Second Piano Concerto,* speaks of the "smoky arpeggios" which arise out of the depths of the piano.[5] Of the dark, murky passage at the beginning of the development of Beethoven's *Ninth Symphony* (first movement), he said, "it remains intensely quiet without crescendo, its periods marked by the distant boom of drums and flashes of red light from the trumpets."[6] It was Tovey, too, who settled once and for all the true nature of form in music, with an unforgettable metaphor: "There are people who talk *a priori* nonsense about the sonata forms, as if these forms were stereotyped moulds into which you shovel your music in the hope that it may set there like a jelly."[7]

None of these examples come from professional music critics. Yet the conductor and the analytical scholar have exemplified that flair for the arresting, the poetic, the imaginative phrase, colored by the glow and warmth of enthusiasm, which is the greatest asset of the practitioner in criticism.

*   *   *

Music criticism is a literary art, and the music critic an essayist with a peculiar responsibility for public service. He would be more accurately called music editor. I am afraid we all think first, and sometimes exclusively, of the music critic as the man who goes to a concert and reports in the morning paper the errors made by the performer the evening before. Wagner's Beckmesser in *Die Meistersinger* is the classic image of the critic. He makes a heavy black mark on his slate for every mistake made either in the composition itself or in the performance of it. Some critics are Beckmessers; others are specialists in the rave review, that most cherished possession of the performer. It is as though praise or damnation, success or defeat, rested entirely in the hands of the man with printers' ink on his fingers. In my opinion, however, the job of passing judgment upon performances is only one quarter of the total responsibility of the music critic. The music editor ought to play four roles, and he ought to play each one of them well. He is, in fact, four persons in one: a reporter, a teacher, a philosopher, and a champion of music in his community.

If the critic would exercise himself continually in all four fields, not only that of judging values, if he would blend them together in his writing and keep them in balance, he could make a vast contribution to the general understanding of music. I cannot agree with Coleridge, who said: "Reviewers are usually people who would have been poets, historians, biographers, &c., if they could: they have tried their talents at one or at the other, and have failed; therefore they turn critics."[8] This may be the natural reaction of the creator to the critic; for, in the words attributed to Homer: "The man who acts the least upbraids the most."[9] But Homer and Coleridge were looking at the little man among the critics. The great critic is not a second-class citizen among artists, but an artist himself.

Louis Lyons has said that all writing is based on reporting. "Whether you are writing history or any kind of article, the first thing is to get the facts straight, and not only straight but as full and detailed, as specific, as vivid, as colorful, as meaningful, as they are. That is, get the story in all its dimensions." Mr. Lyons cited the New England historian, Francis Parkman, the first of whose Journals describes a

trip up Mount Washington. "He wrote it down in the fresh-
ness of his first experience, and captured every sensation,
every fact, every bit of interest, every crumb of information
that came out of the trip. It fascinated him. It excited him.
It filled him with a new crop of facts. It gave him a zest for
the mountain and forests and the life out of doors, and he
writes these feelings in his notes."[10]

Every concert ought to be a Mount Washington. There
is no such thing as a routine concert; each has its special
quality, its items of human interest, its musical drama, its
urgency of communication. No two performances, even of
the most familiar music, are ever quite alike. A review of a
concert ought to be a combination of a news story and an
essay on music, but the story comes first. If you were present
at the concert as a listener, you can relive its incidents and
its excitements the next morning; if you were not there,
you can wish that you had been.

I have picked at random two delightful examples of good
reporting. A Boston Symphony concert at Tanglewood,
conducted by Pierre Monteux:

He made his entrance dressed entirely in white, a huge smile
on his face, and was received with an ovation. How the Tanglewood audiences idolize the veteran conductor.

He was in grand form, but when is he not? He gave Mme.
Henriot-Schweitzer a superb accompaniment, and his Tchaikovsky was supple, beautifully planned and perpetually lyric.
It was the performance of an ardent young man who happens to
have the experience of an octogenarian. Such a combination
occurs once or twice in a lifetime.[11]

A Philadelphia Orchestra concert in New York:

Two young members of the Philadelphia Orchestra scored
personal successes when they appeared as soloists with their
orchestra Tuesday night at Carnegie Hall. The work in which
Eugene Ormandy gave them such a chance to shine was the

Brahms *Concerto for Violin and 'Cello.* . . . They were superb partners, and one of the pleasures of the evening was the way in which at the end of the concerto they shook hands. They were like two crack tennis players who, through alertness and the closest sort of team play, had just won a doubles championship. And their colleagues in the orchestra applauded them heartily.[12]

In the same area of vivid and colorful reporting, but a far cry from ordinary newsprint, is a remarkable account of a performance of one of Beethoven's last quartets, those strangely moving works which take us into a world of sound quite unique and transcendentally beautiful.

Then any one might, if he came by, have observed the *power of music.* For the people were as if asleep or dead—relaxed—some with open sightless eyes, as if they had been slain with great violence and suddenness. An arm in an awkward position; no grace left to these mere bodies. Indeed, a passer-by would have been amazed if he were unacquainted with such causes. . . . A very small child came from the field and started with fright, seeing all asleep or dead. At the turn of the melody, some of the dead shed tears, in respect for Ludwig Beethoven brought in his 52nd year to such a turn of the melody. Music looses the soul so flow the tears.[13]

*   *   *

If the music critic is first a reporter, he is next a teacher. As a member of the editorial staff he has an educational responsibility; as a musician he has the unique opportunity to address the widest public and to contribute, day by day, week by week, to the better understanding of his mysterious art. No conventional teacher in school, college, or conservatory reaches an audience so extensive and so varied.

The critic's sphere of operations is larger than the mere reviewing of concerts. He is an editor in charge of a music page, which should include, as well as reviews—essays, news of the music world, articles written in preparation for concerts, biographical and analytical studies, introductions to new music—all these in judicious mixture and attractive balance. Such an opportunity and challenge calls for a subtle combination of first-class reporting, just evaluation, and persuasive education. If the newspapers would allot enough space for such a concept of the role of music editor, and make the job attractive enough to command the services of the most distinguished critics, there would be less misunderstanding of music and musical problems.

Leaving aside the controversial issues in music—standards in the schools and churches, activities of the unions, the state of opera in America, and others which belong to the critic in his role as champion of music—I should like to cite a few instances of superlatively good teaching, combined with and disguised by reviewing. Examples could be drawn from great critics of the past and present—Robert Schumann in the *Neue Zeitschrift für Musik,* John Sullivan Dwight in *Dwight's Journal of Music,* Ernest Newman in the *Sunday Times,* Richard Aldrich in the *New York Times,* Alfred Frankenstein in the *San Francisco Chronicle,* and Paul Henry Lang in the *New York Herald Tribune.* But I shall draw on the files of the old *Boston Transcript* and its fascinating critic H.T.P., Henry Taylor Parker. His music page set a standard unequaled since his day, even in the metropolitan papers. There was news of music the world around; there were articles on new and old music, and preparatory discussions of significant concerts about to be given in the next few days.

Most of the larger orchestras provide program notes with excellent essays, and many recital programs contain notes on the music, but one cannot read them until one arrives at the hall, which leaves the shocking alternative of perusing them during the performance. The *Transcript* prepared the listener several days ahead, informing the mind and whetting the appetite. Is it restriction of space or lack of initiative that has led to the almost total disappearance of this fine practice?

Parker was always teaching, and it was in his regular reviews that he exhibited his most unusual gift for reporting, evaluating, and educating, all in one. Judgment, criticism, information, appreciation, *joie*, and *élan* combined to make each review a diverting miniature in his unique rhetorical style. Ostensibly evaluating the work of two undergraduate accompanists at a concert of the Harvard Glee Club, he gave his readers an insight into the nature of the fine art of accompanying, and a penetrating glimpse of Bach, Musorgsky, and Irish folk songs.

Pleasurable incidents diversified the concert of the Harvard Glee Club at Symphony Hall last evening—incidents out of routine on such occasions. At the end of Brahms' *Rhapsody*, with a quasi-orchestral background, Mr. Woodworth . . . directed the applause toward Mr. Ramseyer, one of the accompanists; while the audience, quickening its clapping, might have had in mind also his colleague, Mr. Beverage. Jointly and severally, they had excelled, and were to excel, in one of the minor arts that the Glee Club fosters. Clear and crisp, they played the accompaniment to a Chorale from Bach's "Christmas Oratorio" with musicians' feeling for a part within the whole. Now, a piano is an instrument of limitations; yet at their hands, in the pauses of the choir, it crystallized Bach's devout simplicity. Again, in an Irish folk-song, they were unerringly light-fingered, soft-voiced and rhythmical. A 'reduction' for piano is far enough from the tonal pomp of Musorgsky and Rimsky in the "Coronation Scene" of "Boris Godunov." Yet at the paired hands of Mr. Ramseyer and Mr. Beverage the bells sounded; the trumpets made proclamation; the great chords strode and clamored. After many days, to be pianist to the Glee Club has also compensations.[14]

A glittering performance of Mendelssohn's *Italian Symphony* under Koussevitzky was reported only by inference and implication in a little essay on that remarkable genius of twenty-four who had this, his Fourth, in his portfolio when he went to London to conduct the Royal Philharmonic Society!

The secret of all Mendelssohn's surviving pieces is workmanship. . . . Every stroke shall be as clear as the day; fall in the exact place at the due moment; arise from its predecessor, give birth to its successor, whet every perceptive faculty in reader or hearer; leave single unescapable impression. Not one shall exceed; not one fall short; not one be wasted, uncertain, obscure. . . .

This is the perfection of the Mendelssohn of the better overtures, the Italian and the Scotch Symphonies, the music to "A Midsummer Night's Dream." The hearer sits holden before transparencies and euphonies, shadings measured to the breadth of a hair, accents fine and clean as a rapier-edge, phrases never once unshapen, unerring choice of voices be they fiddles, flutes, or drums; the intuition—as it seems—by which all these miracles are accomplished.[15]

On Palestrina's *Stabat Mater:*

The moderns would dramatize the scene, enforce the quickened emotions. For Palestrina, both generate a music of contemplation, beginning in pity, rising into petition, entreaty, final rapture, a music singularly clear and open, sweet and calm, simple and direct (as it seems) to hear, yet subtle in means to ends; a music in which the voices steal in, mount one upon another, climb and swell into ultimate bliss and beatitude; a music in incessant motion among the parts, not wanting poignancy, yet wrapped in an aloof beauty.[16]

H.T.P.'s lineal descendant in Boston is not a critic but the editor, these many years, of the Program Books of the Boston Symphony Orchestra, John N. Burk. For felicity of phrase, deep penetration into the music, and gifted teaching without lectern or podium, he has no equal.

On Brahms and the *Third Symphony:*

Certainly Brahms never wrote a more unspectacular, personal symphony. In six years' pause [between the Second and the

Third], the composer seemed to have taken stock of himself. The romantic excesses which he had absorbed from Beethoven and Schumann, he toned down to a fine, even glow, which was far truer to the essential nature of this self-continent dreamer from the north country. The unveiled sentiment to which, under the shadow of Beethoven, he had been betrayed in the slow movement of his First Symphony, the open emotional proclamation of its final pages; the Schumannesque lyricism of the Second Symphony, its sunlit orchestration and clear, long-breathed diatonic melody, the festive trumpets of its Finale— these inherited musical traits were no longer suitable to the now fully matured symphonic Brahms. His brass henceforth was to be, if not sombre, at least subdued; his emotionalism more tranquillized and *innig;* his erstwhile folklike themes subtilized into a more delicate and personal idiom. In other words, the expansive, sturdy, the militantly bourgeois Brahms, while outwardly unchanged, had inwardly been completely developed into a refined poet quite apart from his kind, an entire aristocrat of his art.[17]

One of the most mysterious relations in music-making is that of a conductor and orchestra, especially when both are virtuosi—the one as the leader, and the many as his equals in their own right. No more delicately balanced cooperative venture exists among human organisms. Mysterious also is the fact that in this work-a-day world of musical performance there comes, rarely and without warning, a transcendent occasion, when through some extraordinary and unpredictable combination of circumstances, not at all understood by listeners or players, the act of musical re-creation reaches the highest pinnacle of near perfection. Such a moment when the fire burned brightest was a performance of the *Eroica Symphony* at Tanglewood.

What mysterious alchemy transmuted the conductor, the players, into pure gold? Perhaps it was that the concert produced a perfect exposition of the leadership principle as applied to the interpretation of great music. Munch was commanding and in full control, but this was no dictatorship of the baton. . .

Each section—the strings, the woods and the brass, produced the cohesion of a fine chamber ensemble. And all the sections consciously and knowingly responded to each other with a precision and balance that was a joy to behold and hear.

As the Beethoven symphony continued, Mr. Munch almost ceased to be the leader. Rather it seemed that peers and equals were all engaged in a joint venture of high significance and great value. It is not certain that all the hearers knew exactly what was taking place on stage. But all sensed the magnitude and splendor of the performance.[18]

One of the permanent areas of misunderstanding about music, an area which will bear repeated efforts at clarification, is its dual nature: on the one hand, the sounds alone, and on the other, their "exquisite meanings."[19] Some people see all music as a description or delineation of something— an event, an idea, a landscape, an emotion; others look upon such music as a lower form of creation, and talk glibly about pure and absolute music. Below are three brief statements about abstract, nondelineative music, one by a specialist, the other two by nonmusicians. I give them as examples of the art of teaching, as examples of that area of music journalism which we look for almost in vain in the daily press.

The first, by John Vincent, touches on the nature of the classical symphony.

A symphony is a kind of musical drama in which there are no players other than musical themes. . . . The characters are musical characters. The incidents which occur are musical incidents, the climaxes and denouments are musical. In short, in a symphony, there are no forces extraneous to the music which influence its course.[20]

What could be clearer?

My next quotation comes from a most unlikely source for

music instruction, a sermon at morning prayers in the Harvard Chapel. But the preacher was J. Edgar Park, sometime President of Wheaton College, a man who never missed a symphony concert, and who had remarkable gifts both as a teacher and as a poet-preacher.

Music in the arts occupies the same position as mathematics does in the sciences. Music is not an expression of ideas so much as the source of ideas.

The best you can *say* about music is to say that it is motion; much of our pleasure in music consists in anticipating where we are going, and our delighted surprise at the composer's most excellent way of getting there.

The motion of the best second-class music is that of swimming or floating like oil on water, the best first-class music moves by walking or running, slowly, or with the speed of light. You swim, for instance in Wagner and in many of the moderns, mesmerized in the flood of tone; but in first-class music you advance step by step on firm ground of which you are intellectually aware.[21]

One can say of music, as did Whitehead of the Periclean ideal, that it is "action weaving itself into a texture of persuasive beauty."[22] The pattern of the texture may be exposition, development, and recapitulation in the normal first movement of the classical symphony. It may be a theme and variations, or a rondo, or a fugue. It is a pattern of sounds in motion. Nothing here about landscape or events or even emotions. Walter Piston said of his music: "It is not intended to convey other than musical thoughts."[23]

Another vast territory of music, however, *does* convey thoughts other than musical thoughts—the *Eroica*, the *Pastoral Symphony*, the entire realm of music with words—representative, delineative music. It is equally important, equally valid. The distinction between these two areas is misunderstood by great numbers of the new population of music listeners. It is one of many problems in listening, to which the critic-as-teacher might well address himself, not once but repeatedly, both in preliminary articles, and in concert reviews.

*   *   *

If the critic as teacher and as reporter is sometimes hardly discernible, there is no one who does not recognize the critic as judge. Value judgments lie in the area of philosophy, especially aesthetics. The profound realization that criticism is a philosophical act is the secret of real stature in the critic. The art of judging literary productions and works of visual art is simpler than the evaluation of music. In music it is necessary, first of all, to recognize two areas of judgment often mixed together. The first is the composer and the second the performer.

It goes without saying that the critic should be acquainted with the score. This should always be possible, except for first performances of manuscript works; and even there the enterprising critic will find a way. Nevertheless, musical notation is one of the most inexact of sciences. There is a story that, during a rehearsal of the Brahms *Piano Quintet* with the Flonzaley Quartet, Harold Bauer settled a dispute by saying "When in doubt, play what's written." But in a deeper sense this didn't really settle anything, for there must always be a variety of interpretations of "what is written." Musical notation has a long and complicated history from the earliest times to our own day. There have been varying degrees of exactness in the notation of musical sound and rhythm, but it is the unique problem and, in another sense, the glory of music, that an interpreter, another personality besides the composer, is necessary and essential to the transaction. It should be clear to the critic, and it should repeatedly be made clear to the public, whether the writer is passing judgment upon the composer and his music or upon the performer and his re-creation and interpretation of the music. At a deeper level, the mysterious relation between the two should be one of the permanent subjects of musical criticism.

First judgments about new music are notoriously bad. This is true of the verdicts of listeners as well as of professional writers. How many times have I walked into the lobby after the performance of a new piece and heard on one side that it was the most magnificent new work of the last decade, and on the other that it was absolutely worthless, "an insult to the listeners"! The immediate reaction has its importance: does the work hold our attention? But final judgment demands fuller acquaintance. When asked for an opinion immediately after the performance of a new work, I must normally answer, "I don't know; I want to hear it again." We need to reserve our judgment, and to hope for a series of repetitions, which, due to the exigencies of program planning over a full concert season, we rarely get.

The qualifications of the critic as judge—and here I am thinking of amateur as well as professional critics—are: curiosity about all music, new and old; eagerness; a questing spirit; humility; tolerance; patience; and persistence in the everlasting attempt to understand the language and the grammar and then to penetrate beneath the surface to those inner sonorities that touch the mind and the heart as well as the ear.

The critic must try to understand the complexities involved in programming, rehearsing, and scheduling performances of music. To give an absurd example: a college newspaper printed a scathing criticism of Mr. Munch and the Boston Symphony for making cuts in the performance of the St. Matthew Passion at a regular pair of subscription concerts. The young man who wrote the article was probably not aware that a complete performance takes upwards of four hours, that the afternoon concert would have lasted from 2:15 until, not 4:00, but 6:00; and the Saturday evening performance until well after midnight. A complete performance of the *St. Matthew Passion* and similar large works, requires an extra "festival" concert with a special time schedule—preferably a division into two sessions, one in the afternoon and the other in the evening, with a dinner intermission. I am tempted to say that half the criticism of programs and concerts comes from a naïve misunderstanding of the complex problems of scheduling, of rehearsing, soloists, the use of the hall, and other special requirements —the logistics of the operation of musical performance. This is another area in which clarification by the music critic could be of real assistance to the general public.

The critic-as-judge assumes a solemn responsibility. We had an example in an American city of unremitting censorious criticism of a symphony conductor, which at long last disaffected the public, alarmed the trustees, and caused the departure of the conductor, who quickly regained a splendid reputation in Europe. A perpetual soul-searching problem for the critic is the evaluation of the work of the young performer in a debut recital. A mere catalogue of errors has little to recommend it. The inchworm technique which moves through the concert, piece by piece, awarding an "A" here and an "E" there, and averaging the whole thing up at the end, seems quite the wrong approach. Such a review reminds me all too keenly of the old-fashioned type of school examination—the performer gets 7 out of 10 points on his first piece, 5 out of 10 on number 2, 0 on number 3, 10 out of 10 on number 4, and so on. The reviewer has missed the point altogether. No wonder the editor is not interested in giving more newspaper space to that sort of writing! Far better devote the available space to a more general estimate which would bring into bold relief one or two main principles for the education of the reading public, and for the thoughtful consideration of the performer himself.

The critic should look upon the performer as a colleague. Both are servants of a great art. If they disagree, let it be in a climate where each respects the other. The performer has one inescapable obligation: to play music "in the style," whether it be Bach or Mozart or Webern or Copland. In the case of old music, this means to re-create in modern times and with modern instruments, not necessarily the letter of the law but the spirit of the law. Style criticism is the most rewarding vein for the critic to exploit. It applies not only to the re-creation of old music but to the music of the nineteenth century and the latest works in the contemporary idiom. In style criticism the batteries of musicology, scholarship, technical knowledge, and common sense must combine to illuminate the perplexing problems of musical performance. When the journalist has the capacity to write as style critic, both performer and public are his beneficiaries.

The music journalist should aim at a balanced judgment and avoid scathing criticism, reserving his thunderbolts for the most egregious violations of good taste in composition or performance. Mere inadequacy is a lesser sin. He should heed the admonition of T. S. Eliot: "The critic may on occasion be called upon to condemn the second-rate and expose the fraudulent: though that duty is secondary to the duty of discriminating praise of what is praiseworthy."[24]

* * *

The fourth role of the critic is that of a champion of music and of all good causes in music, especially on the local scene. He cannot evade the responsibility of taking a stand. He is an editor; and, as his paper shapes its editorial policy fearlessly on the issues of politics, economics, municipal government, highways, taxes, parking, and graft, so the music editor must speak out just as boldly on issues in the musical life of his community and of the nation—music in the schools and the churches, the community orchestra, the community chorus, the opera workshop, the young artist, the operation of the musicians' unions, the controversies over the role of government in the arts, and the misuse of music as a background.

Contemporary music is a good cause. American composers need discriminating support and sympathetic elucidation. I do not mean that every new work is a masterpiece; but I do mean that never before in the history of music has an intelligent public made up of the patrons and lovers of music so neglected or harassed their contemporary composers. We do not hear them gladly, nor do we hear them repeatedly, which is the only way to begin to understand or to form a balanced judgment on their work. The music editor ought never to rest in his persistent effort to illuminate the dark and confusing areas of contemporary music.

Finally, the music critic must keep before the public the desperate human need for music and for the arts in this tense and tragic age, and the simple fact that music is more than relaxation and entertainment. It is a stimulation to the imagination, a consolation of the heart, and a regeneration of the human spirit. It can and does save souls.

✿ POSTLUDE: THE
RECEPTIVE LISTENER

THE THEME of the listener has recurred throughout these pages like the repeated entries of the subject in a fugue. My whole book is oriented in his direction, and the cardinal question for radio, recordings, schools, colleges, the composer, the scholar, the critic, and the performer is—how well have they served the listener? Turn the coin, and we ask of the listener—is he passive or active, unheeding or receptive to beauty? The crisis of music in our generation may well be the question whether millions of citizens have become so accustomed to perpetual background sounds that they have lost the power or the interest to listen.

Like drama, music requires an alert audience. At the opening of a new theater, Archibald MacLeish pointed out that "it is even possible for novelists to write novels only the initiated can decipher. But a play without a participating audience is simply not a play. The stage, even in its proscenium days, was never comprehended within the three inward dimensions but always had the fourth of the attending consciousness. . . . The playwright's task and the actor's and the director's and the designer's is to *hold* that necessary attention."[1] Stravinsky writes of "the listener who gives himself up to the working out of the music—participating in and following it step by step." And he adds: "This exceptional participation gives the partner such lively pleasure that it unites him in a certain measure with the mind that conceived and realized the work to which he is listening, giving him the illusion of identifying himself with the creator. That is the meaning of Raphael's famous adage: To understand is to equal."[2]

The greatest joys of my life have been to make music and to listen to music. I make no distinction between the two. The unforgettable experiences that came to me during a quarter of a century as conductor of the Harvard Glee Club and the Radcliffe Choral Society in the performance of music with young people, have been equaled by unforgettable hours of listening. In a very real sense, listening is the most important experience in music. The basic event of the musical act is hearing, not making; listening, not performing. Performers forget this. Singers are often so concerned with breath control and head resonance, and pianists with the next scale in octaves, that they fail to hear what they sing and play. The best listeners among performers are the string quartet players, for, in that most subtle of all the ensemble arts, each player listens to the other three and, at each instant of performance, to the total sound of all four.

Good listening is not limited to professional musicians. Many amateurs are better listeners than many professionals —more active, more gifted, more penetrating. "Receptiveness to beauty" and "activity of thought" are not the necessary prerogatives of the specialist, but of the alert ear and the lively mind, wherever they may be found.

Concern for the nonperforming listener is a peculiarly American phenomenon. No European college or university has courses similar to our large introductory survey of music for the amateur; yet there is hardly a college in the United States that does not consider such an offering a necessary part of its curriculum. Extension courses on music are unknown abroad, and no European cities have lending libraries of phonograph recordings. If we started late in the race for culture, and without the advantage of centuries of musical inheritance that surround the Italians, the Ger-

mans, the French, the Bohemians, the Russians, and the
English, at least we are doing our best to make up for lost
time.

Music requires not only active listening but repeated
listening. This is because music is in ceaseless motion,
always vanishing, disappearing round the corner, out of
your reach before you can get a hold on it. I often envy my
colleagues in the art department who can, with the use of
slides or with the object itself, examine in detail a painting
or statue. The art object obligingly stays put, whereas music
runs away from us at every instant. I recall a lecture in
which the speaker compared a statue of the Middle Ages
with a statue from the German Baroque, using two slides
side by side on the screen. He examined in detail the hands
of each of the statues, looking from one to the other, then
the drapery, then the face, while our observation shifted
constantly back and forth from detail to detail. Imagine
trying to compare in a similar way two pieces of music.
You can stand before a painting as long as you like, and you
can reread a passage in a book until you understand it. To
listen once and once only to a new or difficult piece of music
is like viewing an art gallery from a motor car.

In music there is no substitute for repetition. The listener
must rehearse the music, as the performers do, by going back
over the difficult, the interesting, and the beautiful passages.
That has been my practice, not only in classroom teaching,
but in a radio program called "Tomorrow's Symphony"
which was inaugurated more than ten years ago when the
educational radio station in Boston, WGBH-FM, began to
broadcast the regular concerts of the Boston Symphony
Orchestra. "Tomorrow's Symphony" is neither commentary
nor program notes but a rehearsal in detail for listeners,
using recordings and selecting only enough passages to
allow for ample repetition.

The Juilliard Quartet has often held public rehearsals of Bartok quartets on college campuses, following the same procedure, and commanding the rapt attention of the student listeners. In the winter of 1961–62 the New York chapter of the International Society for Contemporary Music organized "seminars in listening to new music," at one of which, for example, Roger Sessions supervised a rehearsal of his *String Quintet* (1958). Such live performances have the inestimable advantage of allowing the texture of the music to be examined vertically, strand by strand, violin and cello, then viola alone, and so on; but a recording permits similar scrutiny phrase by phrase, paragraph by paragraph—provided the listener will take the trouble to repeat his record, section by section. "The sensation of the music itself," which Stravinsky called "an indispensable element of investigation,"[3] is available to all those fortunate enough to have a phonograph and records, and it can be repeated time after time, with increasing understanding and enjoyment. Twentieth-century technology has provided the means, but the principle is as old as art. William Byrd laid down the maxim in *Psalmes, Songs, and Sonnets: some solemne, others joyfull, framed to the life of the words.*

A song that is well and artificially made cannot be well perceived nor understood at the first hearing, but the oftner you shall heare it, the better cause of liking you will discover; and commonly that Song is best esteemed with which our eares are best acquainted.[4]

* * *

The ear and, if possible, the eye need constant exercise in developing a musical sense. A score is of great assistance. Do not say you cannot read music; you learn to read by reading. Follow in your score the shape of the melodies, the changes in dynamics, the succession of orchestral choirs and instrumental solos, as they are caught by the ear in full flight; and you will find the whole operation fascinating. Continued practice with recordings yields new facility and new insights. With or without score, bring to your listening the sharpest ears, the keenest attention, and "activity of thought."

Listen first of all for repetitions in the music. Much of the form and structure of a work depends upon the repetition of musical ideas, sometimes identical restatements, sometimes repetitions with changes of orchestration or of dynamics, often no more than changes of register, up an octave or down an octave.

Listen for the nuggets of musical material that are shorter than a whole phrase, the atoms of musical ideas, like the first four notes of the *Fifth Symphony* of Beethoven, the first two notes of the *Ninth Symphony,* the first two notes of Brahms' *Fourth,* the first four notes of the Finale of Mozart's *Jupiter.* Then listen for the manipulation of these fragmentary motifs as they are developed and spun out into great tapestries of sound.

Listen for the objectives or points of arrival. Some are large objectives and some are small. The technical word is cadences, and the sense of approaching such points of arrival is often the first clue to an understanding of architecture in music.

Listen for the interlocking of spans, the end of one idea or passage and the beginning of another. These are sometimes points of cleavage in music, severing musical sentences and paragraphs from each other, but more often they mark the most marvelous welding of ideas, points of articulation at which the listener arrives, only to be swept forward irresistibly into the next span. No two are alike; there is infinite variety in the joiner's art.

These are only a few aspects of what to listen for in the

structure and organization of music. There are other key components besides structure. Listen to the texture of string-quartet writing, the beauty of interwoven strands. Listen to the variegated types of virtuosity for the soloist in concertos. Listen to the fascinating range of sonorities in the orchestra, and in the more limited but equally beautiful timbre of the *a cappella* choir. Listen to the imitative entries of polyphonic music, and the powerful structures erected on the firm foundation of a *passacaglia* bass. Listen to the decorative art of embellishment and coloration, and to the exquisite patterns of tracery in the variations. The aim of all detailed analytical listening is simply the sharpening of aural sensitivity.

As there is a difference for the performer between rehearsal and concert, so there are two kinds of listening—that which challenges the utmost concentration and the utmost energy of penetration, and that which relaxes in effortless attention. Let no one imagine that my intent would be to make all listening an aural and mental gymnastic! The listener will strike his own balance, remembering the universal law of art that the more practice in concentration and precision, the more facets of understanding and beauty suffuse the state of effortless attention.

Music is of all degrees of complexity. Some music is imperious in its demand for complete concentration; anything less is near sacrilege. Other music is diverting or unashamedly functional—the serenades, divertimentos, birthday music, tower music, madrigals (though not all of them), processional music, and even the fascinating changes on the bells, which ring out unceasingly on Sunday mornings from English spires. The gifted listener will draw the distinction between that music which resists the background with all the force of its being, and that which was designed to mingle with the sounds of nature as an accompaniment to other human occupations.

Participation in the making of music contributes enormously to the awareness of the listener. If you are an instrumentalist, take every opportunity to play in a quartet, in chamber music, in an orchestra. If you are a singer, give yourself the delight and the exercise of choral singing, preferably in a chorus or madrigal group which does not read too readily at sight, but moves slowly enough to allow the beauty of the music to reveal itself gradually through repeated rehearsal. If you are a pianist of modest ability, make a collection of easy pieces to play for your own satisfaction and solace—easy Mozart, easy Bach, easy Chambonnières, easy Schumann, easy Bartok. Four-hand music is an everlasting delight; explore the original literature of piano duets by Mozart, Schubert, and others, as well as the arrangements of orchestral scores.

As a final homely suggestion for the listener, make a collection of favorite recordings, those which speak most directly "from the heart to the heart." It may be the *Archduke Trio,* or a Monteverdi madrigal, or the Bartok *Concerto for Orchestra,* or "Domine Deus" from the Bach *Mass,* or the *Diabelli Variations,* or a Mozart Piano Concerto. You may have a special love for landscape music— the *Pastoral Symphony* of Beethoven or Vaughan Williams, Wagner's *Flying Dutchman Overture,* Mendelssohn's *Hebrides Overture, La Mer* by Debussy, the "Scène aux Champs" from *Symphonie Fantastique,* or the "Scène d'Amour" from *Roméo et Juliette;* the pastoral music of the Baroque period such as the Symphony from Bach's *Christmas Oratorio* and from Handel's *Messiah;* or the wonderful nature music of the madrigals, so close to Shakespeare. You will return to this music all your life, and discover new beauties with each hearing.

*   *   *

What are the qualities of mind which characterize the gifted listener? I recognize six, and they are quite remote from the syllabus of facts, topics, and concepts which make up the normal study course in music appreciation. First of all, the mind of the gifted listener is one which becomes naturally active in the presence of music. Music engages his intellect as immediately and directly as his senses and his emotions. In the quaint phrase of Robert Burton's *Anatomy of Melancholy* (1621), music "erects the mind and makes it nimble."[5] When music starts, the listener is "no longer anything but expectation and attention."[6] He knows how to listen, and something about what to listen for. He knows that he cannot hear and remember everything the first time, but he is not bored by repetitions. He welcomes the opportunity to listen again, and again, and again.

Second, he has a feeling for music in history, and some notion of the vastness of music literature, from Gregorian Chant to twelve-tone compositions and beyond. He is aware of the great traditions, the major artistic and aesthetic currents which sweep back and forth through the history and the literature of music. He is sensitive to the great polarities of music, the conflict between classic and romantic, between descriptive, delineative music and that which is not intended to convey other than musical ideas. His mind is not stocked with scraps of information, anecdotes, and unrelated items of inert fact; but he recognizes music as one of the great streams flowing through the history of Western civilization, a channel of insight into the mind of man. The awareness of history will make the listener realize that, in some sense, there is nothing new under the sun. For example, the intricacies of twelve-tone music and of other twentieth-century practices are denounced as "cerebral." Yet this term of opprobrium signifies in reality that the music is the combined product of the mind, the ingenuity, and the technician. Composers from the Middle Ages to the twentieth century have been interested in intellectual music. If Piston and Schönberg are cerebral, so were Bach and Okeghem and the isorhythmic motet. There is no reason why Monteverdi and Berlioz and Beethoven, and Purcell and Richard Strauss and Aaron Copland should not write delineative, pictorial music; but there is also no reason why Stravinsky and Sessions and Carter and Piston should not write music which is strongly a product of the mind, the ingenuity, and the technician. The direct and the simple is condemned by the snobs, and the intricate and involved by the sentimentalists. There is beauty in both, and both are as old as music itself. Furthermore, the intellect of the apprehending listener must join that of composer and performers in the arena of musical combat. The question about many a difficult and involved score is not "Is it good music?" but "Are you up to it?"

The mind of the intelligent listener will exhibit an everlasting curiosity about music, especially new music. He will be tolerant of music he does not at first understand and he will not make up his mind about it, nor condemn it to his friends and to the public, until he has heard it more than once. He will welcome all experiments, from the now old-fashioned cacophony of the *Rite of Spring* to Boulez and Stockhausen and electronic music. One must never forget the lady who, looking at the painting of a sunset by Turner, said, "Why, Mr. Turner, I never saw a sunset like that," to which Turner replied: "Madam, don't you wish you had?" The uneducated listener interprets music through his prejudices, his feelings, and his emotions. The educated listener is able to balance these subjective reactions against a more objective sense of style, a knowledge of structure, form, and movement, and a more acute sense of sound. Tolerance of the new and strange should lead, with each repetition, to a measure of understanding and to the only true basis for evaluation.

The listener will acquire gradually that most precious quality: taste. Implicit in taste is the recognition of standards of value and of stature in music, a sense of artistic rightness, about Bach, Mozart, Stravinsky, Copland, and Piston. Taste comes only through prayer and fasting. It is the philosopher's gift. Its enemies are, on one side, ignorance, and on the other, snobbism. Breadth of knowledge of the history and literature of the art is its best friend.

The fifth characteristic of the listener is an awareness of the infinite varieties of beauty. Beauty in music is not only pleasant sound and euphonious harmony. There is the sheer beauty of form and of abstract patterns of sound. There are beauties of craftsmanship, the sure-footed fugue, the wonders of invertible counterpoint, the complexities of the manipulation and transformation of musical ideas in a Beethoven symphony. There are beauties of rhythm and motion—the infinite divisibility of a slow beat in *adagios,* the perpetual motion of the *prestos,* the fascinating irregularities of rhythm in Stravinsky, the incomparable waltz and minuet, pavane and galliard. There are beauties of texture and of dissonance and of timbre. The piano, the harpsichord, the clavichord, and the organ—all are keyboard instruments, but each has its basic tone quality within which are subtle gradations, and not so subtle contrasts, from the "glassy sonority" of Copland's *Piano Quartet,*[7] through Stravinsky's *martellato,* to the pianistic *bel canto* of Chopin. There is the bright, rich sonority of violins and the darker, cooler sonority of the viols. The palette of orchestral colors, developed between Berlioz and Mahler, is seemingly interminable in its extensions. Even the comparatively limited monochromatic sound of the *a cappella* chorus has, in the hands of a skillful conductor, a multitude of sonorous effects.

The diversities of beauty are endless. I have called the roll of some score of composers in several categories, and the lists might be extended at random. Each composer has his specialties, and if you are to enjoy and understand his music you must respond to it *in its own terms.* Bartok is an example. His music is dissonant, complex, barbaric in rhythm, fantastically weird in sonorities. Yet these very qualities, along with his intense seriousness and utter directness of statement, have attracted young and old, professional and amateur, in common admiration. A love of Mozart does not rule out an equal passion for Bartok.

Finally, the gifted listener will be deeply aware of the inexhaustible communicative and regenerative powers of music. So great are these powers in some music that those who listen are never the same again. The late works of Beethoven belong to such a special territory in the world of beauty—the *Ninth Symphony,* the *Missa Solemnis,* the last piano sonatas, the *Diabelli Variations,* and the last string quartets. The inner sonorities are even more remarkable than the outer sonorities. There is a growing introspection, a deepening of insight, a concern for the philosophical and the spiritual. Beethoven is preoccupied not only with new forms of music but with new ideas—gratitude, thanksgiving, contemplation, the unattainable, the mystical, the ethereal. There is a basic aesthetic and spiritual ambiguity about music. You cannot tell what it means, as you can tell what words mean. But making all the most extreme allowances for such ambiguity, hundreds and hundreds of people from Beethoven's time to our own have been convinced beyond all doubt that in the Variations of Opus 97 and Opus 111, and in the last quartets, Beethoven was speaking directly to them; and the discourse was of something sublime, eternal, heavenly, and pure in heart.

Great art is timeless, and its power of communication and regeneration is as true and contemporary today as the day it was written. The Greek tragedies, Shakespeare, Goethe and Bach, Byrd and Beethoven speak immediately, urgently, and unmistakably to us. We listen, and we are changed. Whenever and wherever that experience occurs —solitary in a crowded concert hall, or alone with a record player—we find in it an "habitual vision of greatness."[8] That vision is free and open to all, makers of music or listeners, professionals or amateurs. For those who are truly receptive, the world of music is an imperishable world of order and of beauty.

NOTES · INDEX

❧ NOTES

PRELUDE

1. Harriette K. Smith, *History of the Lowell Institute* (Boston: Lawson, Wolffe, 1898), p. 48.

2. From the first stanza of "Fair Harvard," *The Harvard Song Book*, 5th ed., rev. (Cambridge, Mass.: The Harvard Glee Club, 1922), p. 1.

3. A. N. Whitehead, *The Aims of Education* (London: Williams and Norgate, 1932), p. 1.

CHAPTER I · MUSIC: BACKGROUND OR ART?

1. "U.S. Events Listed for Music Season," *New York Times,* November 19, 1960, p. 42.

2. Artemus Ward (pseud. of Charles Farrar Browne), *His Travels* (New York: Carleton, 1866), p. 73. In Chapter X, "Boston," Artemus Ward recounts the sights and wonders of the city— the "hoss cars," the "skool sistim," and Harvard College "pleasantly situated in the Bar-room of Parker's," but everyone he meets asks him if he has seen the "Grate Orgin." "Summin up," he says, "Mr. Reveer, whose tavern I stop at, informed me that it can be distinctly heard through a smoked glass in his nativ town in New Hampshire, any clear day."

3. See Thomas E. Noonan, "Selling Discs on Subscription," *New York Times,* March 20, 1960, Sec. II, p. 17.

4. I have been told by Irving Lowens of the Library of Congress that, although it is impossible to keep "withdrawn" records on the shelves or even order them through local dealers (on account of the paper work involved in the system of regional distributors), such records are available and may be ordered by writing direct to the Educational Department of the manufacturer which originally issued the records.

See also David Hall, "The Nonavailable Recording," *Music Educators Journal* (September–October 1963), pp. 136–138.

5. It was sad to read on page 31 of the *New York Times,* May 27, 1963, that "concerts by the New York Philharmonic, on nation-

wide radio each week for 33 years, have been dropped by the Columbia Broadcasting System."

6. Robert Taylor, "Twain Held Muzak Pioneer" from "The Roving Eye," *Boston Herald*, September 29, 1960, p. 33.

7. Quoted in Stephen C. Clapp, "The Turn of the Screw," *Harvard Crimson*, 138(75):2 (May 16, 1960).

8. *New York Times*, February 11, 1960, pp. 1, 58.

9. *New York Times*, February 8, 1961, p. 24.

10. Letter from Professor William F. Russell to author, September 10, 1959.

11. Described in the *Herald Tribune* (New York), July 13, 1962, p. 8.

12. *Daily Tribune* (Chicago), December 29, 1959.

13. Conversation with the author.

14. Ernest Earnest, "Must the TV Technicians Take Over the Colleges?," *Bulletin of the American Association of University Professors* 44(3):582 (September 1958).

15. Letter to Hartford N. Gunn from E. G. Cohen, January 20, 1959.

16. Reported in the *Christian Science Monitor*, June 2, 1960, p. 13.

17. Ps. 115:6.

18. Igor Stravinsky, *Poetics of Music*, trans. Arthur Knodel and Ingolf Dahl (Cambridge, Mass.: Harvard University Press, 1947), p. 76.

19. Alfred North Whitehead, *Science and the Modern World* (New York: Macmillan, 1948), p. 290.

CHAPTER II · SCHOOLS, COLLEGES, AND CONSERVATORIES

1. See Allen P. Britton, "Music Education: An American Specialty," in P. H. Lang, ed., *One Hundred Years of Music in America* (New York: G. Schirmer, 1961), pp. 211 ff.

2. The Concord Series of Music and Books on the Teaching of Music (Boston: E. C. Schirmer Music Company, 1919–   ).

3. Jacques Barzun, *Teacher in America* (Boston: Little, Brown, 1945), p. 121. The omission noted by Mr. Barzun was corrected in 1962 by a dissertation (unpublished) at the University of Michigan by Charles W. Heffernan, "Thomas Whitney Surette: Musician and Teacher."

4. For Davison's description of "musical realism" see A. T. Davison, "Music in the Boston Public Schools," *Harvard Musical Review*, 2:3–5 (February 1914).

5. News release prepared by Yale University News Bureau, June 28, 1963.

6. Mimeographed script prepared for Radio Station WTIC, New Haven, and available through Yale University News Bureau; Yale Reports No. 65, THE PLACE OF MUSIC IN EDUCATION, IV, "Music in Secondary Schools" (April 7, 1957).

7. Floy Little Bartlett, *Historical Song Miniatures for Children*, No. 3, "Haydn," published in Schmidt's Educational Series (Boston: Arthur P. Schmidt, 1922); reprinted with the kind permission of Sidney F. Bartlett.

8. *Ibid.*, No. 5, "Beethoven."

9. Unsigned article, "Desirability Ratings of Personality Items Show Individual Differences," *ETS Developments* (Princeton, N.J.: Educational Testing Service, 1960), vol. 8, no. 3 (April 1960).

10. Thomas Munro, "The Interrelation of the Arts in Secondary Education" in *The Creative Arts in American Education* (Cambridge, Mass.: Harvard University Press, 1960), pp. 18, 19.

11. Mimeographed statement prepared for A TWO-DAY CONFERENCE on "Music in the Secondary School," based on recommendations by members of the Summer Institute for High School Music Teachers, Bennington College, August 1–2, 1962, pp. 2, 3, 4.

12. Whitehead, *Aims of Education*, p. 1.

13. James Bryant Conant, *The American High School Today: A First Report to Interested Citizens* (New York: McGraw-Hill, 1959), p. 48. The italics are Mr. Conant's.

14. James Bryant Conant, *Recommendations for Education in the Junior High School Years* (Princeton, N.J.: Educational Testing Service, 1960), p. 46.

15. Britton, "Music Education: an American Specialty," p. 216.

16. This *rapprochement* is possibly the most significant aspect of the Yale Music Seminar organized by the Office of Science and Technology and the Office of Education in 1963. See p. 28.

17. It is interesting that the founding of the conservatories at St. Petersburg and Moscow and the Hochschule für Musik in Berlin fell within the same decade as the Peabody Conservatory in Baltimore and the New England Conservatory in Boston. Harrison Keller points out that "the European conservatory system was one which divorced music study entirely from other educational procedures and confined such music studies to the academy where liberal arts subjects were not required, nor were they even offered." H. Keller, *Address* on the occasion of the 100th Anniversary of the Peabody Institute at Baltimore, February 1957 (Boston: New England Conservatory of Music, 1957), pp. 4, 5.

18. David D. Boyden *et al.*, "Report of the A.B. Committee,"

Bulletin of the National Association of Schools of Music, 42:9–12 (January 1957).

19. The Harvard Glee Club, the Radcliffe Choral Society, the University Choir, and the Harvard-Radcliffe Orchestra.

20. Institute of Higher Education, *Liberal Education and Engineering* (1961), reported in "Illiberal Engineers," *New York Times,* January 29, 1961, sec. IV, p. 9.

21. Whitehead, *Aims of Education,* p. 29. See also Chapter VII, page 152.

22. Conant, *American High School Today,* p. 96.

23. Whitehead, *Science and the Modern World,* p. 291.

CHAPTER III · MUSIC IN CHURCHES

1. V. A. Yzermans, ed., "Inter Plurimas Pastoralis: Motu Proprio on the Restoration of Sacred Music," *All Things in Christ: Encyclicals and Selected Documents of Saint Pius X* (Westminster, Md.: Newman Press, 1954), pp. 196–206. For the text of the Motu Proprio, see also Nicolas Slonimsky, *Music Since 1900,* 2nd ed. (New York: W. W. Norton, 1938), pp. 523–529; and *The White List* of the Society of St. Gregory of America (Glen Rock, N.J., 1961), pp. 3–7.

2. Sister Mary Theophane, O.S.F., "Organotes," in *Catholic Music Educators Bulletin,* 5(3):4 (December 1952).

3. See Paul Hume, "Music in Church," *America,* 95(7):194 (May 19, 1956).

4. *Ibid.*

5. *The English Hymnal* (London: Oxford University Press, 1906), Preface: "The Music," by R. Vaughan Williams, pp. x–xi.

6. Heb. 11:32.

7. Archibald T. Davison, *Protestant Church Music in America* (Boston: E. C. Schirmer, 1933); Archibald T. Davison, *Church Music: Illusion and Reality* (Cambridge, Mass.: Harvard University Press, 1952).

8. *The Pilgrim Hymnal,* 9th ed. (Boston: Pilgrim Press, 1963), "Preface to the Music," p. vii.

9. "Proposed Declaration of Principles," Potomac Clericus, Episcopal Diocese of Virginia, comp. L. P. Beveridge, Chairman of Committee on Music, 1957.

10. William Beveridge, "A Discourse on Church Music," in *Thesaurus Theologicus or a Complete System of Divinity* (Oxford: J. Parker, 1816), II, 362.

11. I Cor. 14:15.

12. See Chapter I.

13. Edward Murray, "A Twentieth Century Folk Mass," *Harvard Crimson,* 137(8):2 (February 10, 1959).

14. *Canon Law Revision,* 1959, Sec. B.20 (29), "Of the Hymns, Anthems, and Music of the Church" (London: Society for Promoting Christian Knowledge, 1960).

15. *Annotated Constitution and Canons for the Government of the Protestant Episcopal Church in the United States of America,* 2nd ed., rev. Jackson A. Dykman (Greenwich, Conn.: Seabury Press, 1954), p. 420.

16. See also *Old Organs in Present-Day Churches:* A handbook for churches which have old tracker organs (Methuen, Mass.: Andover Organ Co., 1962).

17. *The Pilgrim Hymnal,* "Preface to the Music," p. vii.

18. A. C. Lovelace and W. C. Rice, *Music and Worship in the Church* (Nashville: Abingdon Press, 1960), p. 151.

19. Thomas Morley, *A Plaine and Easie Introduction to Practicall Musicke* (London: Peter Short, 1597), p. 179. There is a facsimile reproduction as a "rare text illustrating life and thought in Shakespeare's England," ed. Canon E. H. Fellowes, for the Shakespeare Association, 1937. See also a modern edition, ed. R. Alec Harman (New York: W. W. Norton, 1952), pp. 292, 293.

20. Matt. 10:16.

21. Job 38:7.

CHAPTER IV · THE ARTS AND GOVERNMENT

1. Reported in Ralph Purcell, *Government and Art: A Study of American Experience* (Washington, D.C.: Public Affairs Press, 1956), p. 128.

2. *New York Times,* March 14, 1961, p. 32.

3. Brooks Atkinson, "Congressional Objection to Aid for the Arts," *New York Times,* January 23, 1962, p. 30.

4. *Ibid.*

5. Nan Robertson, "Musicians' Plight in U.S. Deplored," *New York Times,* November 16, 1961, p. 41.

6. *International Musician* (Official Journal of the American Federation of Musicians), 59(7):7 (January 1961).

7. Frank Thompson, "Government and the Arts," in Lang, ed., *One Hundred Years of Music in America,* p. 262.

8. Nan Robertson, "Musicians' Plight," p. 41.

9. Harold Weston, "The Arts and the Sword of Damocles," *1962 NCAG Annual Report* (New York: National Council on the Arts in Government, 1962), p. 2.

10. Robert Sabin, "Government and the Arts," *Musical America,* 82(1):18 (January 1962).

11. Jack Gould, "Federal Role in the Arts (television review)," *New York Times,* February 13, 1961.

12. Nan Robertson, "Musicians' Plight," p. 45.

13. Purcell, *Government and Art.*

14. Frank Thompson, "Remarks at the Sixty-fourth Annual Convention of the American Federation of Musicians," Atlantic City, N.J., June 13, 1961, reported in *International Musician,* 59(12):44 (June 1961).

15. Keller, *Address,* pp. 2, 3.

16. National Council on the Arts and Government, *1962 NCAG Annual Report,* p. 4.

17. *Ibid.,* pp. 6–8.

18. A list of ANTA recommendations is to be found in Sabin's article in *Musical America.*

19. Thompson, "Government and the Arts," p. 277.

20. Published in full in the *New York Times,* December 15, 1961, p. 40.

21. Sabin, "Government and the Arts," p. 17.

CHAPTER V · COMPOSER AND PUBLIC

1. Rudyard Kipling, "The Explorer," in *Rudyard Kipling's Verse, Inclusive Edition* (New York: Doubleday Page, 1924), p. 120.

2. Aaron Copland, "At the Thought of Mozart," *Boston Symphony Orchestra Programs* (1955–1956), February 3–4, 1956, pp. 761–762; reprinted from *High Fidelity Magazine* (January 1956).

3. Igor Stravinsky, *Oedipus Rex,* Full Score, 1948 Revision (London: Edition Russe de Musique—S. et N. Koussewitzky, 1949), p. 85.

4. Pierre Lalo, article in *Le Temps,* June 3, 1913; quoted in Slonimsky, *Music Since 1900,* p. 138.

5. Melville Clark, "Development of New Musical Instruments" (part of a mimeographed proposal for an Institute of Scientific Research in Music at Harvard University, May 1962), p. 1.

6. Milton Babbitt, "Electronic Music," *Princeton Alumni Bulletin* (April 22, 1960), p. 9.

7. Donald F. Tovey, *Essays in Musical Analysis* (London: Oxford University Press, 1935), I, 68.

8. Paul Fromm, "The Princeton Seminar—Its Purpose and Promise," *The Musical Quarterly,* 46(2):156 (April 1960).

9. Unpublished remarks by Milton Babbitt at a Panel Discussion, "The Place of Music in Our Future Society," held in connection with the dedication of the Paul Creative Arts Center, University of New Hampshire, October 14, 1960.

10. Aaron Copland, *Music and Imagination* (Cambridge, Mass.: Harvard University Press, 1952), p. 8.

11. *Boston Symphony Orchestra Programs* (1940–1941), October 18–19, 1940, p. 86.

12. Mark DeWolfe Howe, ed., *The Occasional Speeches of Justice Oliver Wendell Holmes* (Cambridge, Mass.: Harvard University Press, 1962), pp. 6, 7.

13. *Webster's New International Dictionary*, 2nd ed. (Springfield, Mass.: G. and C. Merriam, 1947), II, 2505.

14. Quoted in Andrew Heath, "Music of the Future: An Open Letter to Audiences" (four-page pamphlet distributed at Mr. Heath's piano recitals).

15. *Sunday Herald* (Boston), November 3, 1957, sec. III, p. 8.

16. I Thess. 5:21.

CHAPTER VI · THE PERFORMER

1. Matt. 25:14–30.

2. *New York Times*, September 2, 1962, sec. II, p. 9.

3. "Major Grants for Young Artists," *Musical America*, 80(5):13 (April 1960).

4. *New York Times*, February 27, 1961, p. 24.

5. Howard Taubman, "Choral Blues," *New York Times*, April 24, 1960, sec. II, p. 11.

6. Hyman Faine, "The American Guild of Musical Artists and the Non-Professional Chorus," *Bulletin of the American Choral Foundation*, 1(3):3 (January 1959).

7. "AGMA Unfair Tag Faces NY Symph," *Variety*, November 25, 1955.

8. Letter from Edward Tatnall Canby, *New York Times*, July 30, 1961, sec. II, p. 7.

9. Walter Piston, "Teaching as a Composer's Craft," *The Composer's News Record*, 9:1, 2 (Spring 1949).

10. *Ibid.*, p. 2.

11. A more complete discussion of this subject will be found in the forthcoming book by Alan Rich, *Careers and Opportunities in Music* (New York: E. P. Dutton, 1964).

CHAPTER VII · SCHOLAR AND TEACHER

1. Charles Burney, *A General History of Music from the Earliest Ages to the Present Period*, 4 vols. (London, 1776–1789); ed. Frank Mercer, 2 vols. (New York: Dover Publications, 1957).

2. Carl G. A. von Winterfeld, *Johannes Gabrieli und sein Zeitalter* (Berlin: Schlesinger'sche Buch- und Musikhandlung, 1834).

3. For full details on these and other scholarly publications, see Willi Apel, "Editions, Historical," *Harvard Dictionary of Music* (Cambridge, Mass.: Harvard University Press, 1944), pp. 226–234.

4. From informal remarks by Max Loehr, introducing his Inaugural Lecture as Abby Aldrich Rockefeller Professor of Oriental Art at Harvard, February 24, 1961.

5. C. Hubert H. Parry, *Studies of Great Composers,* 8th ed. (London: George Routledge and Sons, 1904), p. 15.

6. Waldo S. Pratt, "On Behalf of Musicology," *The Musical Quarterly,* I(1):16 (1915).

7. W. Oliver Strunk, "The State and Resources of Musicology in the United States," *American Council of Learned Societies Bulletin,* no. 19 (Washington, D.C.: American Council of Learned Societies, December 1932).

8. J. A. Fuller Maitland, ed., *The Works of Henry Purcell* (London: Novello, Ewer, 1893), "To the Reader," preface to vol. 5: "Twelve Sonnatas of Three Parts."

9. Pratt, "On Behalf of Musicology," p. 10.

10. Reprint from *Courses and Degrees,* 1962–63, Stanford University, p. 275.

11. W. S. Gilbert and Arthur Sullivan, *The Gondoliers* (New York: G. Schirmer, 1941), Act II, no. 16, p. 212.

12. Whitehead, *Aims of Education,* pp. 27–30.

13. John Livingston Lowes, *The Road to Xanadu* (London: Constable and Co., 1927), p. 4.

14. *Ibid.,* pp. 58, 59, 63, 4. Lowes's quotation (p. 63, repeated on p. 103) is from Coleridge, ed. J. Shawcross, *Biographia Literaria* (Oxford, 1907), I, 202.

15. *Ibid.,* p. 59.

CHAPTER VIII · THE MUSIC CRITIC

1. Virgil Thomson, "The Art of Judging Music," in *Music and Criticism: A Symposium,* ed. Richard F. French (Cambridge, Mass.: Harvard University Press, 1948), p. 113.

2. Stravinsky, *Poetics of Music,* p. 87.

3. Alfred Einstein, *Mozart, His Character, His Work,* trans. Arthur Mendel and Nathan Broder (New York: Oxford University Press, 1945), p. 302.

4. Aaron Copland, *What to Listen for in Music,* rev. ed. (New York: McGraw-Hill, 1957).

5. Donald F. Tovey, *Essays in Musical Analysis,* vol. III: *Concertos* (London: Oxford University Press, 1936), p. 122.

6. Tovey, *Essays,* vol. II: *Symphonies (II)* (1935), p. 16.

7. *Ibid.,* p. 18.

8. Samuel Taylor Coleridge, *Lectures and Notes on Shakspere and Other English Poets* (London: George Bell and Sons, 1893), p. 36.

9. Quoted in "Topics," *New York Times,* March 22, 1960, p. 36.

10. Louis M. Lyons, "Words and Writing," *Nieman Reports,* 9:20–23 (January 1955).

11. *New York Times,* July 20, 1959, p. 15.

12. *New York Times,* January 6, 1960, p. 31.

13. Paul Goodman, "A Ceremonial," in *Spearhead: Ten Years' Experimental Writing in America* (New York: James Laughlin, 1947), pp. 139–140.

14. *Boston Evening Transcript,* December 11, 1925, p. 8. Both the undergraduates mentioned by H.T.P. have had notable careers in music—Lowell P. Beveridge (Beverage in the review) as Organist and Choirmaster of Columbia University and now a clergyman and member of the faculty of the Virginia Theological Seminary, and Frank W. Ramseyer as Professor of Music at Wheaton College, Norton, Mass.

15. *Boston Evening Transcript,* December 23, 1927, p. 9.

16. *Boston Evening Transcript,* April, 25, 1930, p. 10.

17. *Boston Symphony Orchestra Programs* (1962–1963), April 11–13, 1963, p. 1488.

18. *Sunday Herald* (Boston), July 24, 1960, sec. I, p. 8.

19. "I hear not the volumes of sound merely—I am moved by the exquisite meanings." Walt Whitman, "That Music Always Round Me," *Leaves of Grass* (Philadelphia: David McKay, 1900), p. 398.

20. John Vincent, "The *Sinfonia India* of Carlos Chavez" (unpublished radio script), p. 6.

21. J. Edgar Park, unpublished Sermon delivered in the Harvard Chapel, March 2, 1951.

22. Alfred North Whitehead, *Adventures of Ideas* (New York: Macmillan, 1933), p. 65.

23. From a note by Piston on the first performance of his Fourth Symphony, Program Book of the Minneapolis Symphony Orchestra, March 30, 1951.

24. T. S. Eliot, "Frontiers of Criticism," *Sewanee Review,* 64(4):540 (1956).

POSTLUDE: THE RECEPTIVE LISTENER

1. *Harvard Crimson,* 138(109):R3 (October 14, 1960).
2. Stravinsky, *Poetics of Music,* p. 134.
3. *Ibid.,* p. 26.
4. William Byrd, Preface: "To all true lovers of Musicke," in *Psalmes, Songs, and Sonnets: some solemne, others joyfull, framed to the life of the words: Fit for Voyces or Viols* (London: Thomas Snodham, 1611); reprinted in *The English Madrigal School,* ed. E. H. Fellowes (London: Stainer and Bell, 1920), XVI, vii.
5. Robert Burton (Democritus Junior), *The Anatomy of Melancholy,* 3 vols. (Boston: William Veazie, 1859), II, 227.
6. Paul Claudel, *The Eye Listens;* quoted by Aaron Copland in *Music and Imagination,* p. 10.
7. The phrase *"ff* (sempre) glassy sonority" is found in the score of the piano part of Aaron Copland, *Quartet for Piano and Strings* (New York: Boosey and Hawkes, 1952), p. 7.
8. Whitehead, *Aims of Education,* p. 106.

⚜ INDEX